Eat That Frog!

Eat That Frog!

21 Great Ways to Stop Procrastinating and Get More Done in Less Time

Brian Tracy

First published in Great Britain in 2004 by Hodder & Stoughton
An Hachette UK company

Revised paperback edition by Yellow Kite in 2017
An imprint of Hodder & Stoughton
An Hachette UK company

30

A CIP catalogue record for this title is available
from the British Library

Paperback ISBN 978 1 444 76542 7
eBook ISBN 978 1 848 94124 3

Typeset in ITC Stone Serif

Printed and bound in Great Britain by Clays Ltd, Elcograf S.p.A.

Hodder & Stoughton policy is to use papers that are natural, renewable and
recyclable products and made from wood grown in sustainable forests. The
logging and manufacturing processes are expected to conform to the
environmental regulations of the country of origin.

Yellow Kite
Hodder & Stoughton Ltd
Carmelite House
50 Victoria Embankment
London EC4Y 0DZ

www.yellowkitebooks.co.uk
www.hodder.co.uk

To my remarkable daughter Catherine,
an amazing girl with a wonderful mind
and an incredible future lying before her

Contents

Preface

Thank you for picking up this book. I hope these ideas help you as much as they have helped me and thousands of others. In fact, I hope this book changes your life forever.

There is never enough time to do everything you have to do. You are literally swamped with work and personal responsibilities, endless e-mails, social media, projects, stacks of magazines to read, and piles of books you intend to get to one of these days—as soon as you get caught up.

But the fact is that you are *never* going to get caught up. You will never get on top of your tasks. You will never get far enough ahead to be able to get to all those e-mails, books, magazines, and leisure-time activities that you dream of.

And forget about solving your time management problems by becoming more productive. No matter how many personal productivity techniques you master, there will always be more to do than you can ever accomplish in the time you have available to you, no matter how much it is.

You can get control of your time and your life only by changing the way you think, work, and deal with the never-ending river of responsibilities that flows over you each day. You can get control of your tasks and activities only to the degree that you stop doing some things and start spending more time on the few activities that can really make a difference in your life.

I have studied time management for more than forty years. I have immersed myself in the works of Peter Drucker, Alec Mackenzie, Alan Lakein, Stephen Covey, and many, many others. I have read hundreds of books and thousands of articles on personal efficiency and effectiveness. This book is the result.

Each time I came across a good idea, I tried it out in my own work and personal life. If it worked, I incorporated it into my talks and seminars and taught it to others.

Galileo once wrote, "You cannot teach a man anything; you can only help him find it within himself."

Depending upon your level of knowledge and experience, these ideas may sound familiar. This book will bring them to a higher level of awareness. When you learn and apply these methods and techniques over and over until they become habits, you will alter the course of your life in a very positive way.

Learning from Successful People

Let me tell you something about myself and the origins of this little book. I started off in life with few advantages, aside from a curious mind. I did poorly in school and left without graduating. I worked at laboring jobs for several years. My future did not appear promising.

As a young man, I got a job on a tramp freighter and went off to see the world. For eight years, I traveled and worked and then traveled some more, eventually visiting more than eighty countries on five continents.

When I could no longer find a laboring job, I got into sales, knocking on doors, working on straight commission. I struggled from sale to sale until I began looking around me and asking, "Why is it that other people are doing better than I am?"

Then I did something that changed my life. I began to ask successful people what they were doing that enabled them to be more productive and earn more money than me. And they told me. I did what they advised me to do, and my sales went up. Eventually, I became so successful that I was made a sales manager. As a sales manager, I used the same strategy. I asked successful managers what they did to achieve such great results, and when they told me, I did it myself. In no time at all, I began to get the same results they did.

This process of learning and applying what I had learned changed my life. I am still amazed at how simple and obvious it is. Just find out what other successful people do and do the same things until you get the same results. Learn from the experts. Wow! What an idea.

Success Is Predictable

Simply put, some people are doing better than others because they do things differently and they do the right things right. Especially, successful, happy, prosperous people use their time far, far better than the average person.

Coming from an unsuccessful background, I had developed deep feelings of inferiority and inadequacy. I had fallen into the mental trap of assuming that people who were doing better than me were actually better than me. What I learned was that this was not necessarily true. They were just doing things *differently*, and what they had learned to do, within reason, I could learn as well.

This was a revelation to me. I was both amazed and excited with this discovery. I still am. I realized that I could change my life and achieve almost any goal I could set if I just found out what others were doing in that area and then did it myself until I got the same results they were getting.

Within one year of starting in sales, I was a top salesman. A year later I was made a manager. Within three years, I became a vice president in charge of a ninety-five-person sales force in six countries. I was twenty-five years old.

Over the years, I have worked in twenty-two different jobs; started and built several companies; earned a business degree from a major university; learned to speak French, German, and Spanish; and been a speaker, trainer, or consultant for more than 1,000 companies. I currently give talks and seminars to more than 250,000 people each year, with audiences as large as 20,000 people.

A Simple Truth

Throughout my career, I have discovered and rediscovered a simple truth. The ability to concentrate single-mindedly on your most important task, to do it well and to finish it completely, is the key to great success, achievement, respect, status, and happiness in life. This key insight is the heart and soul of this book.

This book is written to show you how to get ahead more rapidly in your career and to simultaneously enrich your personal life. These pages contain the twenty-one most powerful principles on personal effectiveness I have ever discovered.

These methods, techniques, and strategies are practical, proven, and fast acting. In the interest of time, I do not dwell on the various psychological or emotional explanations for procrastination or poor time management. There are no lengthy departures into theory or research. What you will learn are specific actions you can take immediately to get better, faster results in your work and to increase your happiness.

Every idea in this book is focused on increasing your overall levels of productivity, performance, and output and on making you more valuable in whatever you do. You can apply many of these ideas to your personal life as well.

Each of these twenty-one methods and techniques is complete in itself. All are necessary. One strategy might be effective in one situation and another might apply to another task. All together, these twenty-one ideas represent a smorgasbord of personal effectiveness techniques that you can use at any time, in any order or sequence that makes sense to you at the moment.

The key to success is action. These principles work to bring about fast, predictable improvements in performance and results. The faster you learn and apply them, the faster you will move ahead in your career—guaranteed!

There will be no limit to what you can accomplish when you learn how to *Eat That Frog!*

Brian Tracy
Solana Beach, California
January 2017

Introduction: Eat That Frog

This is a wonderful time to be alive. There have never been more possibilities and opportunities for you to achieve more of your goals than exist today. As perhaps never before in human history, you are actually drowning in options. In fact, there are so many good things that you can do that your ability to decide among them may be the critical determinant of what you accomplish in life.

If you are like most people today, you are overwhelmed with too much to do and too little time. As you struggle to get caught up, new tasks and responsibilities just keep rolling in, like the waves of the ocean. Because of this, you will never be able to do everything you have to do. You will never be caught up. You will always be behind in some of your tasks and responsibilities, and probably in many of them.

The Need to Be Selective

For this reason, and perhaps more than ever before, your ability to select your most important task at each moment, and then to get started on that task and to get it done both quickly and well, will probably have more of an impact on your success than any other quality or skill you can develop.

An average person who develops the habit of setting clear priorities and getting important tasks completed quickly will run circles around a genius who talks a lot and makes wonderful plans but who gets very little done.

The Truth about Frogs

It has been said that if the first thing you do each morning is to eat a live frog, you can go through the day with the satisfaction of knowing that that is probably the *worst* thing that is going to happen to you all day long.

Your "frog" is your biggest, most important task, the one you are most likely to procrastinate on if you don't do something about it. It is also the one task that can have the greatest positive impact on your life and results at the moment.

The first rule of frog eating is this:
If you have to eat two frogs, eat the *ugliest* one first.

This is another way of saying that if you have two important tasks before you, start with the biggest, hardest, and most important task first. Discipline yourself to begin immediately and then to persist until the task is complete before you go on to something else.

Think of this as a test. Treat it like a personal challenge. Resist the temptation to start with the easier task. Continually remind yourself that one of the most important decisions you make each day is what you will do immediately and what you will do later, if you do it at all.

The second rule of frog eating is this:
If you have to eat a live frog at all, it doesn't pay
to sit and look at it for very long.

The key to reaching high levels of performance and productivity is to develop the lifelong habit of tackling your major task first thing each morning. You must develop the routine of "eating your frog" before you do anything else and without taking too much time to think about it.

Take Action Immediately

In study after study of men and women who get paid more and promoted faster, the quality of "action orientation" stands out as the most observable and consistent behavior they demonstrate in everything they do. Successful, effective people are those who launch directly into their major tasks and then discipline themselves to work steadily and single-mindedly until those tasks are complete.

"Failure to execute" is one of the biggest problems in organizations today. Many people confuse activity with accomplishment. They talk continually, hold endless meetings, and make wonderful plans, but in the final analysis, no one does the job and gets the results required.

Develop the Habits of Success

Your success in life and work will be determined by the kinds of habits that you develop over time. The habit of setting priorities, overcoming procrastination, and getting on with your most important task is a mental and physical skill. As such, this habit is learnable through practice and repetition, over and over again, until it locks into your subconscious mind and becomes a permanent part of your behavior. Once it becomes a habit, it becomes both automatic and easy to do.

This habit of starting and completing important tasks has an immediate and continuous payoff. You are designed mentally and emotionally in such a way that task completion gives you a positive feeling. It makes you happy. It makes you feel like a winner.

Whenever you complete a task of any size or importance, you feel a surge of energy, enthusiasm, and self-esteem. The more important the completed task, the happier, more confident, and more powerful you feel about yourself and your world.

The completion of an important task triggers the release of *endorphins* in your brain. These endorphins give you a natural "high." The endorphin rush that follows successful completion of any task makes you feel more positive, personable, creative, and confident.

Develop a Positive Addiction

Here is one of the most important of the so-called secrets of success. You can actually develop a "positive addiction" to endorphins and to the feeling of enhanced clarity, confidence, and competence that they trigger. When you develop this addiction, you will, at an unconscious level, begin to organize your life in such a way that you are continually starting and completing ever more important tasks and projects. You will actually become addicted, in a very positive sense, to success and contribution.

One of the keys to your living a wonderful life, having a successful career, and feeling terrific about yourself is to develop the habit of starting and finishing important jobs. When you do, this behavior will take on a power of its own and you'll find it easier to complete important tasks than not to complete them.

No Shortcuts

You remember the story of the man who stops a musician on a street in New York and asks how he can get to Carnegie Hall. The musician replies, "Practice, man, practice."

Practice is the key to mastering any skill. Fortunately, your mind is like a muscle. It grows stronger and more capable with use. With practice, you can learn any behavior or develop any habit that you consider either desirable or necessary.

The Three Ds of New Habit Formation

You need three key qualities to develop the habits of focus and concentration, which are all learnable. They are decision, discipline, and determination.

First, make a *decision* to develop the habit of task completion. Second, *discipline* yourself to practice the principles you are about to learn over and over until they become automatic. And third, back everything you do with *determination* until the habit is locked in and becomes a permanent part of your personality.

Visualize Yourself as You Want to Be

There is a special way that you can accelerate your progress toward becoming the highly productive, effective, efficient person that you want to be. It consists of your thinking continually about the rewards and benefits of being an action-oriented, fast-moving, and focused person. See yourself as the kind of person who gets important jobs done quickly and well on a consistent basis.

Your mental picture of yourself has a powerful effect on your behavior. Visualize yourself as the person you intend to be in the future. Your self-image, the way you see yourself on the inside, largely determines your performance on the outside. All improvements in your *outer* life begin with improvements on the *inside*, in your mental pictures.

You have a virtually unlimited ability to learn and develop new skills, habits, and abilities. When you train yourself, through repetition and practice, to overcome procrastination and get your most important tasks completed quickly, you will move onto the fast track in your life and career and step on the accelerator of your potential.

Eat That Frog!

1

Set the Table

Before you can determine your "frog" and get on with the job of eating it, you have to decide exactly what you want to achieve in each area of your life. *Clarity* is perhaps the most important concept in personal productivity. The number one reason why some people get more work done faster is because they are absolutely clear about their goals and objectives, and they don't deviate from them. The greater clarity you have regarding what you want and the steps you will have to take to achieve it, the easier it will be for you to overcome procrastination, eat your frog, and complete the task before you.

A major reason for procrastination and lack of motivation is vagueness, confusion, and fuzzy-mindedness about what you are trying to do and in what order and for what reason. You must avoid this common condition with all your strength by striving for ever-greater clarity in your major goals and tasks.

> **Here is a great rule for success:**
> **Think on paper.**

Only about 3 percent of adults have clear, written goals. These people accomplish five and ten times as much as people of equal or better education and ability but who, for whatever reason, have never taken the time to write out exactly what they want.

There is a powerful formula for setting and achieving goals that you can use for the rest of your life. It consists of seven simple steps. Any one of these steps can double and triple your productivity if you are not currently using it. Many of my graduates have increased their incomes dramatically in a matter of a few years, or even a few months, with this simple, seven-part method.

Step one: *Decide exactly what you want.* Either decide for yourself or sit down with your boss and discuss your goals and objectives until you are crystal clear about what is expected of you and in what order of priority. It is amazing how many people are working away, day after day, on low-value tasks because they have not had this critical discussion with their managers.

One of the very worst uses of time is to do something very well that need not be done at all.

Stephen Covey says, "If the ladder is not leaning against the right wall, every step we take just gets us to the wrong place faster."

Step two: *Write it down.* Think on paper. When you write down a goal, you crystallize it and give it tangible form. You create something that you can touch and see.

On the other hand, a goal or objective that is not in writing is merely a wish or a fantasy. It has no energy behind it. Unwritten goals lead to confusion, vagueness, misdirection, and numerous mistakes.

Step three: *Set a deadline on your goal; set subdeadlines if necessary.* A goal or decision without a deadline has no urgency. It has no real beginning or end. Without a definite deadline accompanied by the assignment or acceptance of specific responsibilities for completion, you will naturally procrastinate and get very little done.

Step four: *Make a list of everything you can think of that you are going to have to do to achieve your goal.* As you think of new activities, add them to your list. Keep building your list until it is complete. A list gives you a visual picture of the larger task or objective. It gives you a track to run on. It dramatically increases the likelihood that you will achieve your goal as you have defined it and on schedule.

Step five: *Organize the list into a plan.* Organize your list by priority and sequence. List all tasks in the order they need to be done. Take a few minutes to decide what you need to do first and what you can do later. Decide what has to be done before something else and what needs to be done afterward.

Even better, lay out your plan visually in the form of a series of boxes and circles on a sheet of paper, with lines and arrows showing the relationship of each task to every other task. You'll be amazed at how much easier it is to achieve your goal when you break it down into individual tasks.

With a written goal and an organized plan of action, you will be far more productive and efficient than people who are carrying their goals around in their minds.

Step six: *Take action on your plan immediately.* Do something. Do anything. An average plan vigorously executed is far better than a brilliant plan on which nothing is done. For you to achieve any kind of success, execution is everything.

Step seven: *Resolve to do something every single day that moves you toward your major goal.* Build this activity into your daily schedule. You may decide to read a specific number of pages on a key subject. You may call on a specific number of prospects or customers. You may engage in a specific period of physical exercise. You may learn a certain number of new words in a foreign language. Whatever it is, you must never miss a day.

Keep pushing forward. Once you start moving, keep moving. Don't stop. This decision, this discipline alone, can dramatically increase your speed of goal accomplishment and boost your personal productivity.

The Power of Written Goals

Clear written goals have a wonderful effect on your thinking. They motivate you and galvanize you into action. They stimulate your creativity, release your energy, and help you overcome procrastination as much as any other factor.

Goals are the fuel in the furnace of achievement. The bigger your goals and the clearer they are, the more excited you become about achieving them. The more you think about your goals, the greater becomes your inner drive and your desire to accomplish them.

Think about your goals and review them daily. Every morning when you begin, take action on the most important task you can accomplish to achieve your most important goal at the moment.

EAT THAT FROG!

1. Take a clean sheet of paper right now and make a list of ten goals you want to accomplish in the next year. Write your goals as though a year has already passed and they are now a reality.

Use the present tense, positive voice, and first person singular so that they are immediately accepted by your subconscious mind. For example, you could write, "I earn *x* number of dollars per year by this date" or "I weigh *x* number of pounds by this date" or "I drive such and such a car by this date."

2. Review your list of ten goals and select the one goal that, if you achieved it, would have the greatest positive impact on your life. Whatever that goal is, write it on a separate sheet of paper, set a deadline, make a plan, take action on your plan, and then do something every single day that moves you toward that goal. This exercise alone could change your life!

Plan Every Day in Advance

Planning is bringing the future into the present
so that you can do something about it now.
ALAN LAKEIN

You have heard the old question, "How do you eat an elephant?" The answer is "One bite at a time!"

How do you eat your biggest, ugliest frog? The same way: you break it down into specific step-by-step activities and then you start on the first one.

Your mind, your ability to think, plan, and decide, is your most powerful tool for overcoming procrastination and increasing your productivity. Your ability to set goals, make plans, and take action on them determines the course of your life. The very act of thinking and planning unlocks your mental powers, triggers your creativity, and increases your mental and physical energies.

Conversely, as Alec Mackenzie wrote, *"Taking action without thinking things through is a prime source of problems."*

Your ability to make good plans before you act is a measure of your overall competence. The better the plan you have, the easier it is for you to overcome procrastination, to get started, to eat your frog, and then to keep going.

Increase Your Return on Energy

One of your top goals at work should be to get the highest possible return on your investment of your mental, emotional, and physical energy. The good news is that every minute spent in planning saves as many as ten minutes in execution. It takes only about 10 to 12 minutes for you to plan your day, but this small investment of time will save you up to two hours (100 to 120 minutes) in wasted time and diffuse effort throughout the day.

You may have heard of the Six-P Formula. It says, "Proper Prior Planning Prevents Poor Performance."

When you consider how helpful planning can be in increasing your productivity and performance, it is amazing how few people practice it every single day. And planning is really quite simple to do. All you need is a piece of paper and a pen. The most sophisticated Outlook system, computer app, or time planner is based on the same principle. It is based on your sitting down and making a list of everything you have to do before you begin.

Two Extra Hours per Day

Always work from a list. When something new comes up, add it to the list before you do it. You can increase your productivity and output by 25 percent or more—about two hours a day—from the first day that you begin working consistently from a list.

Make your list the night before for the workday ahead. Move everything that you have not yet accomplished onto your list for the coming day, and then add everything that you have to do the next day. When you make your list the night before, your subconscious mind will work on your list all night long while you sleep. Often you will wake up with great ideas and insights that you can use to get your job done faster and better than you had initially thought.

The more time you take to make written lists of everything you have to do, in advance, the more effective and efficient you will be.

Different Lists for Different Purposes

You need different lists for different purposes. First, you should create a *master list* on which you write down everything you can think of that you want to do sometime in the future. This is the place where you capture every idea and every new task or responsibility that comes up. You can sort out the items later.

Second, you should have a *monthly list* that you make at the end of the month for the month ahead. This may contain items transferred from your master list.

Third, you should have a *weekly list* where you plan your entire week in advance. This is a list that is under construction as you go through the current week.

This discipline of systematic time planning can be very helpful to you. Many people have told me that the habit of taking a couple of hours at the end of each week to plan the coming week has increased their productivity dramatically and changed their lives completely. This technique will work for you as well.

Finally, you should transfer items from your monthly and weekly lists onto your *daily list*. These are the specific activities that you are going to accomplish the following day.

As you work through the day, tick off the items on your list as you complete them. This activity gives you a visual picture of accomplishment. It generates a feeling of success and forward motion. Seeing yourself working progressively through your list motivates and energizes you. It raises your self-esteem and self-respect. Steady, visible progress propels you forward and helps you overcome procrastination.

Planning a Project

When you have a project of any kind, begin by making a list of every step that you will have to complete to finish the project from beginning to end. Organize the steps by *priority*, what is most important, and *sequence*, which tasks you must complete in order. Lay out the project in front of you on paper or on a computer-based project planner so that you can see every step and task. Then go to work on one task at a time. You will be amazed at how much you get done in this way.

As you work through your lists, you will feel more and more effective and powerful. You will feel more in control of your life. You will be naturally motivated to do even more. You will think better and more creatively, and you will get more and better insights that enable you to do your work even faster.

As you work steadily through your lists, you will develop a sense of positive forward momentum that enables you to overcome procrastination. This feeling of progress gives you more energy and keeps you going throughout the day.

One of the most important rules of personal effectiveness is the 10/90 Rule. This rule says that the first 10 percent of time that you spend planning and organizing your work before you begin will save you as much as 90 percent of the time in getting the job done once you get started. You only have to try this rule once to prove it to yourself.

When you plan each day in advance, you will find it much easier to get going and to keep going. The work will go faster and smoother than ever before. You will feel more powerful and competent. You will get more done faster than you thought possible. Eventually, you will become *unstoppable*.

EAT THAT FROG!

1. Begin today to plan every day, week, and month in advance. Take a notepad or sheet of paper (or use your smartphone) and make a list of everything you have to do in the next twenty-four hours. Add to your list as new items come up. Make a list of all your projects, the big multitask jobs that are important to your future.

2. Lay out all of your major goals, projects, and tasks by *priority*, what is most important, and by *sequence*, what has to be done first, what comes second, and so forth. Start with the end in mind and work backward.

Think on paper! Always work from a list. You'll be amazed at how much more productive you become and how much easier it is to eat your frog.

3

Apply the 80/20 Rule to Everything

We always have time enough,
if we will but use it aright.

JOHANN WOLFGANG VON GOETHE

The 80/20 Rule is one of the most helpful of all concepts of time and life management. It is also called the "Pareto Principle" after the Italian economist Vilfredo Pareto, who first wrote about it in 1895. Pareto noticed that people in his society seemed to divide naturally into what he called the "vital few," the top 20 percent in terms of money and influence, and the "trivial many," the bottom 80 percent.

He later discovered that virtually all economic activity was subject to this principle as well. For example, this principle says that 20 percent of your activities will account for 80 percent of your results, 20 percent of your customers will account for 80 percent of your sales, 20 percent of your products or services will account for 80 percent of your profits, 20 percent of your tasks will account for 80 percent of the value of what you do, and so on. This means that if you have a list of ten items to do, two of those items will turn out to be worth much more than the other eight items put together.

Number of Tasks versus Importance of Tasks

Here is an interesting discovery. Each of the ten tasks may take the same amount of time to accomplish. But one or two of those tasks will contribute five or ten times the value of any of the others.

Often, a single task can be worth more than all the other *nine* items put together. This task is invariably the *frog* that you should eat first.

Can you guess on which items the average person is most likely to procrastinate? The sad fact is that most people procrastinate on the top 10 or 20 percent of items that are the most valuable and important, the "vital few." They busy themselves instead with the least important 80 percent, the "trivial many" that contribute very little to results.

Focus on Activities, Not Accomplishments

You often see people who appear to be busy all day long but seem to accomplish very little. This is almost always because they are busy working on tasks that are of low value while they are procrastinating on the one or two activities that, if they completed them quickly and well, could make a real difference to their companies and to their careers.

The most valuable tasks you can do each day are often the hardest and most complex. But the payoff and rewards for completing these tasks efficiently can be tremendous. For this reason, you must adamantly refuse to work on tasks in the bottom 80 percent while you still have tasks in the top 20 percent left to be done.

Before you begin work, always ask yourself, "Is this task in the top 20 percent of my activities or in the bottom 80 percent?"

Rule: Resist the temptation to clear up small things first.

Remember, whatever you choose to do over and over eventually becomes a habit that is hard to break. If you choose to start your day working on low-value tasks, you will soon develop the habit of always starting and working on low-value tasks. This is not the kind of habit you want to develop or keep. Low-value tasks are like rabbits; they multiply continually. You never get caught up.

The hardest part of any important task is getting started on it in the first place. Once you actually begin work on a valuable task, you will be naturally motivated to continue. A part of your mind loves to be busy working on significant tasks that can really make a difference. Your job is to feed this part of your mind continually.

Motivate Yourself

Just *thinking* about starting and finishing an important task motivates you and helps you overcome procrastination. The fact is, the time required to complete an important job is often the same as the time required to do an unimportant job. The difference is that you get a tremendous feeling of pride and satisfaction from completing something valuable and significant. However, when you complete a low-value task using the same amount of time and energy, you get little or no satisfaction.

Time management is really *life* management, personal management. It is really taking control of the *sequence of events*. Time management is taking control over what you do next. And you are always free to choose the task that you will do next. Your ability to choose between the important and the unimportant is the key determinant of your success in life and work.

Effective, productive people discipline themselves to start on the most important task that is before them. They force themselves to eat that frog, whatever it is. As a result, they accomplish vastly more than the average person and are consequently much happier. This should be your way of working as well.

EAT THAT FROG!

1. Make a list of all the key goals, activities, projects, and responsibilities in your life today. Which of them are, or could be, in the top 10 or 20 percent of tasks that represent, or could represent, 80 or 90 percent of your results?

2. Resolve today that you are going to spend more and more of your time working in those few areas that can really make a difference in your life and career and spend less and less time on lower-value activities.

4

Consider the Consequences

Every great man has become great,
every successful man has succeeded,
in proportion as he has confined his
powers to one particular channel.
ORISON SWETT MARDEN

The mark of the superior thinker is his or her ability to accurately predict the consequences of doing or not doing something. The potential consequences of any task or activity are the key determinants of how important a task really is to you and to your company. This way of evaluating the significance of a task is how you determine what your next frog really is.

Dr. Edward Banfield of Harvard University, after more than fifty years of research, concluded that a "long time perspective" is the most accurate single predictor of upward social and economic mobility in America. A long time perspective turns out to be more important than family background, education, race, intelligence, connections, or virtually any other single factor in determining your success in life and at work.

Your attitude toward time, your "time horizon," has an enormous impact on your behavior and your choices. People who take a long-term view of their lives and careers always seem to make much better decisions about their time and activities than people who give very little thought to the future.

Rule: Long-term thinking improves
short-term decision making.

Successful people have a clear *future orientation*. They think five, ten, and twenty years out into the future. They analyze their choices and behaviors in the present to make sure that what they are doing today is consistent with the long-term future that they desire.

Make Better Decisions about Time

In your work, having a clear idea of what is really important to you in the long term makes it much easier for you to make better decisions about your priorities in the short term.

By definition, something that is important has long-term potential consequences. Something that is unimportant has few or no long-term potential consequences. Before starting on anything, you should always ask yourself, *"What are the potential consequences of doing or not doing this task?"*

Rule: Future intent influences and
often determines present actions.

The clearer you are about your future intentions, the greater influence that clarity will have on what you do in the moment. With a clear long-term vision, you are much more capable of evaluating an activity in the present to ensure that it is consistent with where you truly want to end up.

Think about the Long Term

Successful people are those who are willing to delay gratification and make sacrifices in the short term so that they can enjoy far greater rewards in the long term. Unsuccessful people, on the other hand, think more about short-term pleasure and immediate gratification while giving little thought to the long-term future.

Denis Waitley, a motivational speaker, says, "Losers try to escape from their fears and drudgery with activities that are tension-relieving. Winners are motivated by their desires toward activities that are goal-achieving."

For example, coming into work earlier, reading regularly in your field, taking courses to improve your skills, and focusing on high-value tasks in your work will all combine to have an enormous positive impact on your future. On the other hand, coming into work at the last moment, reading the newspaper, drinking coffee, and socializing with your coworkers may seem fun and enjoyable in the short term but inevitably leads to lack of promotion, underachievement, and frustration in the long term.

If a task or activity has large potential positive consequences, make it a top priority and get started on it immediately. If something can have large potential negative consequences if it is not done quickly and well, that becomes a top priority as well. Whatever your frog is, resolve to gulp it down first thing.

Motivation requires *motive*. The greater the potential positive impact that an action or behavior of yours can have on your life, once you define it clearly, the more motivated you will be to overcome procrastination and get it done quickly.

Keep yourself focused and forward moving by continually starting and completing those tasks that can make a major difference to your company and to your future.

The time is going to pass anyway. The only question is how you use it and where you are going to end up at the end of the weeks and months that pass. And where you end up is largely a matter of the amount of consideration you give to the likely consequences of your actions in the short term.

Thinking continually about the potential consequences of your choices, decisions, and behaviors is one of the very best ways to determine your true priorities in your work and personal life.

Obey the Law of Forced Efficiency

The Law of Forced Efficiency says, "There is never enough time to do everything, but there is always enough time to do the most important thing." Put another way, you cannot eat every tadpole and frog in the pond, but you can eat the biggest and ugliest one, and that will be enough, at least for the time being.

When you're running out of time and know that the consequences of not completing a key task or project can be really serious, you always seem to find the time to get it done, often at the very last minute. You start early, you stay late, and you drive yourself to complete the job rather than face the unpleasantness that would follow if you didn't complete it within the time limit.

Rule: There will never be enough time to
do everything you have to do.

The average person in business today, especially a manager in the age of cutbacks, is working at 110 to 130 percent of capacity. And the jobs and responsibilities just keep piling up. We all have stacks of reading material we still have to go through. Many people have hundreds of hours of reading and projects backlogged at home and at the office.

What this means is that you will never be caught up. Get that wishful idea out of your mind. All you can hope for is to be on top of your most important responsibilities. The others will just have to wait.

Deadlines Are an Excuse

Many people say that they work better under the pressure of deadlines. Unfortunately, years of research indicate that this is seldom true.[1]

Under the pressure of deadlines, often self-created through procrastination, people suffer greater stress, make more mistakes, and have to redo more tasks than under any other conditions. Often the mistakes that people make when working under tight deadlines lead to defects and cost overruns that cause substantial financial losses in the long term. Sometimes a job actually takes much longer to complete when people rush to get it done at the last minute and then have to redo it.

It is much better to plan your time carefully in advance and then build in a sizable buffer to compensate for unexpected delays and diversions. However much time you think a task will take, add on another 20 percent or more as insurance. Or make a game of getting the job done well in advance of the deadline. You will be amazed at how much more relaxed you are and how much better a job you do when you are on top of your most important tasks.

Three Questions for Maximum Productivity

You can use three questions on a regular basis to keep yourself focused on completing your most important tasks on schedule. The first question is, *"What are my highest-value activities?"* Put another way, what are the biggest frogs that you have to eat to make the greatest contribution to your organization? To your family? To your life in general?

This is one of the most important questions you can ever ask and answer. What are your highest-value activities? First, think this through for yourself. Then, ask your boss. Ask your coworkers and subordinates. Ask your friends and family. Like focusing the lens of a camera, you must be crystal clear about your highest-value activities before you begin work.

The second question you can ask continually is, *"What can I and only I do, that if done well, will make a real difference?"* This question came from the late Peter Drucker, the management guru. It is one of the most important of all questions for achieving personal effectiveness. What can you and only you do that if done well can make a real difference?

This is something that only you can do. If you don't do it, it won't be done by someone else. But if you *do* do it, and you do it well, it can really make a difference to your life and your career. What is this particular frog for you?

Every hour of every day, you can ask yourself this question and come up with a specific answer. Your job is to be clear about the answer and then to start and work on this task before anything else.

The third question you can ask is, *"What is the most valuable use of my time right now?"* In other words, "What is my biggest frog of all *at this moment?"*

This is the core question of time management. Answering this question correctly is the key to overcoming procrastination and becoming a highly productive person. Every hour of every day, one task represents the most valuable use of your time at that moment. Your job is to ask yourself this question, over and over again, and to always be working on the answer to it, whatever it is.

Do first things first and second things not at all. As Goethe said, *"The things that matter most must never be at the mercy of the things that matter least."*

The more accurate your answers are to these three questions, the easier it will be for you to set clear priorities, to overcome procrastination, and to get started on that one activity that represents the most valuable use of your time.

EAT THAT FROG!

1. Review your list of tasks, activities, and projects regularly. Continually ask yourself, "Which one project or activity, if I did it in an excellent and timely fashion, would have the greatest positive consequences in my work or personal life?"

2. Determine the most important thing you could be doing every hour of every day, and then discipline yourself to work continually on the most valuable use of your time. What is this for you right now?

Whatever it is that can help you the most, set it as a goal, make a plan to achieve it, and go to work on your plan immediately. Remember the wonderful words of Goethe: *"Only engage, and the mind grows heated. Begin it, and the work will be completed."*

5

Practice Creative Procrastination

Make time for getting big tasks done every day.
Plan your daily workload in advance. Single out the
relatively few small jobs that absolutely must be
done immediately in the morning. Then go directly
to the big tasks and pursue them to completion.

BOARDROOM REPORTS

Creative procrastination is one of the most effective
of all personal performance techniques. It can change
your life.

The fact is that you can't do everything that you have
to do. You have to procrastinate on *something*. Therefore,
deliberately and consciously procrastinate on small tasks.
Put off eating smaller or less ugly frogs. Eat the biggest
and ugliest frogs before anything else. Do the worst first!

Everyone procrastinates. The difference between high
performers and low performers is largely determined by
what they choose to procrastinate on.

Since you must procrastinate anyway, decide today
to procrastinate on low-value activities. Decide to pro-
crastinate on, outsource, delegate, and eliminate those
activities that don't make much of a contribution to
your life in any case. Get rid of the tadpoles and focus
on the frogs.

Priorities versus Posteriorities

Here is a key point. To set proper priorities, you must set posteriorities as well. A *priority* is something that you do more of and sooner, while a *posteriority* is something that you do less of and later, if at all.

> Rule: You can get your time and your life
> under control only to the degree to which
> you discontinue lower-value activities.

One of the most powerful of all words in time management is the word *no*! Say it politely. Say it clearly so that there are no misunderstandings. Say it regularly as a normal part of your time management vocabulary.

Warren Buffett, one of the richest men in the world, was once asked his secret of success. He replied, "Simple. I just say *no* to everything that is not absolutely vital to me at the moment."

Say no to anything that is not a high-value use of your time and your life. Say no graciously but firmly to avoid agreeing to something against your will. Say it early and say it often. Remember that you have no spare time. As we say, "Your dance card is full."

For you to do something new, you must complete or stop doing something old. Getting in requires getting out. Picking up means putting down.

Creative procrastination is the act of thoughtfully and deliberately deciding upon the exact things you are not going to do right now, if ever.

Procrastinate on Purpose

Most people engage in *unconscious* procrastination. They procrastinate without thinking about it. As a result, they procrastinate on the big, valuable, important tasks that can have significant long-term consequences in their lives and careers. You must avoid this common tendency at all costs.

Your job is to deliberately procrastinate on tasks that are of low value so that you have more time for tasks that can make a big difference in your life and work. Continually review your duties and responsibilities to identify time-consuming tasks and activities that you can abandon with no real loss. This is an ongoing responsibility for you that never ends.

For example, a friend of mine was an avid golfer when he was single. He liked to golf three or four times a week, three to four hours each time. Over a period of years, he started a business, got married, and had two children. But he still played golf three to four times a week until he finally realized that his time on the golf course was causing him enormous stress at home and at the office. Only by abandoning most of his golf games could he get his life back under control. And he did. He cut back to one round of golf per week and transformed his life, especially his home life.

Set Posteriorities on Time-Consuming Activities

Continually review your life and work to find time-consuming tasks and activities that you can abandon. Cut down on television watching and Internet surfing and instead spend the time with your family, read, exercise, or do something else that enhances the quality of your life.

Look at your work activities and identify the tasks that you could delegate or eliminate to free up more time for the work that really counts. Begin today to practice creative procrastination. Set posteriorities wherever and whenever you can. This decision alone can enable you to get your time and your life under control.

EAT THAT FROG!

1. Practice "zero-based thinking" in every part of your life. Ask yourself continually, "If I were not doing this already, knowing what I now know, would I start doing it again today?" If it is something you would not start again today, knowing what you now know, it is a prime candidate for abandonment or creative procrastination.

2. Examine each of your personal and work activities and evaluate it based on your current situation. Select at least one activity to abandon immediately or at least deliberately put off until your more important goals have been achieved.

6

Use the ABCDE Method Continually

The first law of success is concentration—
to bend all the energies to one point,
and to go directly to that point, looking
neither to the right nor to the left.
WILLIAM MATHEWS

The more thought you invest in planning and setting priorities before you begin, the more important things you will do and the faster you will get them done once you get started. The more important and valuable a task is to you, the more likely you will be motivated to overcome procrastination and launch yourself into the job.

The ABCDE Method is a powerful priority setting technique that you can use every single day. This technique is so simple and effective that it can, all by itself, make you one of the most efficient and effective people in your field.

Think on Paper

The power of this technique lies in its simplicity. Here's how it works: You start with a list of everything you have to do for the coming day. Think on paper.

You then place an *A*, *B*, *C*, *D*, or *E* next to each item on your list before you begin the first task.

An "A" item is defined as something that is very important, something that you must do. This is a task that will have serious positive or negative consequences if you do it or fail to do it, like visiting a key customer or finishing a report that your boss needs for an upcoming board meeting. These items are the frogs of your life.

If you have more than one A task, you prioritize these tasks by writing "A-1," "A-2," "A-3," and so on in front of each item. Your A-1 task is your biggest, ugliest frog of all.

"Shoulds" versus "Musts"

A "B" item is defined as a task that you *should* do. But it has only mild consequences. These are the tadpoles of your work life. This means that someone may be unhappy or inconvenienced if you don't do one of these tasks, but it is nowhere as important as an A task. Returning an unimportant telephone message or reviewing your e-mail would be a B task.

The rule is that you should never do a B task when an A task is left undone. You should never be distracted by a tadpole when a big frog is sitting there waiting to be eaten.

A "C" task is defined as something that would be *nice* to do but for which there are no consequences at all, whether you do it or not. C tasks include phoning a friend, having coffee or lunch with a coworker, and completing some personal business during work hours. These sorts of activities have no effect at all on your work life.

A "D" task is defined as something you can *delegate* to someone else. The rule is that you should delegate everything that someone else can do so you can free up more time for the A tasks that only you can do.

An "E" task is defined as something that you can *eliminate* altogether, and it won't make any real difference. This may be a task that was important at one time but is no longer relevant to you or anyone else. Often it is something you continue to do out of habit or because you enjoy it. But every minute that you spend on an E task is time taken away from an A task or activity that can make a real difference in your life.

After you have applied the ABCDE Method to your list, you will be completely organized and ready to get more important things done faster.

Take Action Immediately

The key to making this ABCDE Method work is for you to now discipline yourself to start immediately on your A-1 task and then stay at it until it is complete. Use your willpower to get going and stay going on this one job, the most important single task you could possibly be doing. Eat the whole frog and don't stop until it's finished completely.

Your ability to think through and analyze your work list and determine your A-1 task is the springboard to higher levels of accomplishment and greater self-esteem, self-respect, and personal pride. When you develop the habit of concentrating on your A-1, most important, activity—on eating your frog—you will start getting more done than any two or three people around you.

EAT THAT FROG!

1. Review your work list right now and put an *A*, *B*, *C*, *D*, or *E* next to each task or activity. Select your A-1 job or project and begin on it immediately. Discipline yourself to do nothing else until this one job is complete.

2. Practice this ABCDE Method every day for the next month on every work or project list before you begin work. After a month, you will have developed the habit of setting and working on your highest-priority tasks, and your future will be assured!

Focus on Key Result Areas

When every physical and mental resource is focused, one's power to solve a problem multiplies tremendously.
NORMAN VINCENT PEALE

"Why am I on the payroll?" This is one of the most important questions you can ever ask and answer, over and over again, throughout your career.

As it happens, most people are not sure exactly why they are on the payroll. But if you are not crystal clear about why you are on the payroll and what results you have been hired to accomplish, it is very hard for you to perform at your best, get paid more, and get promoted faster.

In simple terms, you have been hired to get specific results. A wage or a salary is a payment for a specific quality and quantity of work that can be combined with the work of others to create a product or service that customers are willing to pay for.

Your job can be broken down into about five to seven key result areas, seldom more. These represent the results that you absolutely, positively have to get to fulfill your responsibilities and make your maximum contribution to your organization.

A key result area is defined as something for which you are completely responsible. If you don't do it, it doesn't get done. A key result area is an activity that is under your control. It produces an output that becomes an input or a contributing factor to the work of others.

Key result areas are similar to the vital functions of the body, such as those indicated by blood pressure, heart rate, respiratory rate, and brain-wave activity. An absence of any one of these vital functions leads to the death of the organism. By the same token, your failure to perform in a critical result area of your work can lead to the end of your job as well.

The Big Seven in Management and Sales

The key result areas of management are planning, organizing, staffing, delegating, supervising, measuring, and reporting. These are the areas in which a manager must get results to be successful in his or her area of responsibility. A weakness in any one of these areas can lead to underachievement and failure as a manager.

The key result areas of sales are prospecting, building rapport and trust, identifying needs, presenting persuasively, answering objections, closing the sale, and getting resales and referrals. Poor performance in any one of these key skills can lead to lower sales and sometimes the failure of a salesperson.

Whatever you do, you must have certain essential skills for you to do your job in an excellent fashion. These demands are constantly changing. You have already developed core competencies that make it possible for you to do your job in the first place. But certain key results are central to your work and determine your success or failure in your job. What are they?

Clarity Is Essential

The starting point of high performance is for you to identify the key result areas of your work. Discuss them with your boss. Make a list of your most important output responsibilities, and make sure that the people above you, on the same level as you, and below you are in agreement with it.

For example, for a salesperson, getting qualified appointments is a key result area. This activity is the key to the entire sales process. Closing a sale is also a key result area. When the sale is made, it triggers the activities of many other people to produce and deliver the product or service.

For a company owner or key executive, negotiating a bank loan may be a key result area. Hiring the right people and delegating effectively are both key result areas. For a receptionist or secretary, typing letters and answering the phone and transferring callers quickly and efficiently are defined as key result areas. People's ability to perform these tasks quickly and efficiently largely determines their pay and promotability.

Give Yourself a Grade

Once you have determined your key result areas, the second step is for you to grade yourself on a scale of one to ten (with one being the lowest and ten being the highest) in each of those areas. Where are you strong and where are you weak? Where are you getting excellent results and where are you underperforming?

> Rule: Your *weakest* key result area sets the height at which you can use all your other skills and abilities.

This rule says that although you could be exceptional in six out of your seven key result areas, poor performance in the seventh area will hold you back and determine how much you achieve with all your other skills. This weakness will act as a drag on your effectiveness and be a constant source of friction and frustration.

For example, delegating is a key result area for a manager. This skill is the key leverage point that enables a manager to manage and to get results through others. A manager who cannot delegate properly is held back from using all his or her other skills at the maximum levels of effectiveness. Poor delegation skills alone can lead to failure in the job.

Poor Performance Produces Procrastination

One of the major reasons for procrastination in the workplace is that people avoid jobs and activities in those areas where they have performed poorly in the past. Instead of setting a goal and making a plan to improve in a particular area, most people avoid that area altogether, which just makes the situation worse.

The reverse of this is that the *better* you become in a particular skill area, the more motivated you will be to perform that function, the less you will procrastinate, and the more determined you will be to get the job finished.

The fact is that everybody has both strengths and weaknesses. Refuse to rationalize, justify, or defend your areas of weakness. Instead, identify them clearly. Set a goal and make a plan to become very good in each of those areas. Just think! You may be only one critical skill away from top performance at your job.

The Great Question

Here is one of the greatest questions you will ever ask and answer. "What one skill, if I developed and did it in an excellent fashion, would have the greatest positive impact on my career?"

You should use this question to guide your career for the rest of your life. Look into yourself for the answer. You probably know what it is.

Ask your boss this question. Ask your coworkers. Ask your friends and your family. Whatever the answer is, go to work to bring up your performance in this area.

The good news is that all business skills are learnable. If anyone else is excellent in that particular key result area, this is proof that you can become excellent as well, if you decide to.

One of the fastest and best ways to stop procrastinating and get more things done faster is for you to become absolutely excellent in your key result areas. This can be as important as anything else you do in your life or your career.

EAT THAT FROG!

1. Identify the key result areas of your work. What are they? Write down the key results you have to get to do your job in an excellent fashion. Give yourself a grade from one to ten on each one. And then determine the one key skill that, if you did it in an excellent manner, would help you the most in your work.

2. Take this list to your boss and discuss it with him or her. Invite honest feedback and appraisal. You can only get better when you are open to the constructive input of other people. Discuss your conclusions with your staff and coworkers. Talk them over with your spouse.

Make a habit of doing this analysis regularly for the rest of your career. Never stop improving. This decision alone can change your life.

8

Apply the Law of Three

Do what you can, with what you have,
where you are.

THEODORE ROOSEVELT

Three core tasks that you perform contain most of the value that you contribute to your business or organization. Your ability to accurately identify these three key tasks and then to focus on them most of the time is essential for you to perform at your best. Let me tell you a true story.

Three months after her first full-day coaching session with me in San Diego, Cynthia told the group a story: "When I came here ninety days ago, you claimed that you would show me how to double my income and my time off within twelve months. This sounded completely unrealistic, but I was willing to give it a try.

"On the first day, you asked me to write down a list of everything that I did over the course of a week or a month. I came up with seventeen tasks that I was responsible for. My problem was that I was completely overwhelmed with work. I was working ten to twelve hours per day, six days per week, and not spending enough time with my husband and my two young children. But I didn't see any way out.

"I had been working for eight years for a fast-growing entrepreneurial company in the high-tech area, but there always seemed to be an overwhelming amount of work to do and never enough time."

One Thing All Day Long

She continued with her story. "Once I had made this list, you told me to ask this question: 'If you could do only one thing on this list all day long, which *one* task would contribute the greatest value to your company?' Once I had identified that task, which was quite easy, I put a circle around that number.

"You then asked, 'If you could do only one more thing on your list of key tasks, which would be the *second* activity that contributes the most value to your company?'

"Once I had identified the second most important task, you asked me the same question with regard to the *third* most important task.

"You then said something that shocked me at the time. You said that fully 90 percent of the value that you contribute to your company is contained in those three tasks, whatever they are. Everything else you do is either a support task or a complementary task that could probably be delegated, downsized, outsourced, or eliminated."

Take Immediate Action

Cynthia continued with her story. "As I looked at the three tasks, I realized that these were the three things I did that contributed the most value to my company. This was on a Friday. On Monday morning at ten o'clock, I met with my boss and explained what I had discovered. I said that I needed his help in delegating and outsourcing all my work except those three key tasks. I felt that if I could work on those three tasks exclusively, all day long, I could more than double my contribution to the company. Then I told him that if I doubled my contribution, I would like to be paid twice as much."

She said, "My boss was completely silent. He looked at my list of key tasks, looked back up at me, and looked at the list again.

"He then said, 'You're right. These are the three most important things that you do in this company—and the three things that you do best. I will help you delegate and outsource all these other minor tasks to free you up to work full-time on these three key tasks. And if you double your contribution, I will pay you twice as much.'"

Transform Your Life

Cynthia concluded her story by saying, "He did; then I did; then he did. He helped me delegate and assign my minor tasks so I could concentrate on my top three jobs. As a result, I doubled my output over the next thirty days, and he doubled my income.

"I had been working very hard for more than eight years, and I doubled my income in just one month by focusing all my time and energy on my three key tasks. Not only that, but instead of working ten- and twelve-hour days, I work from eight o'clock to five o'clock and spend time in the evenings and on the weekends with my husband and my children. Focusing on my key tasks has transformed my life."

Perhaps the most important word in the world of work is *contribution*. Your rewards, both financial and emotional, will always be in direct proportion to your results, to the value of your contribution. If you want to increase your rewards, you must focus on increasing the value of what you do. You must dedicate yourself to contributing more results to your company. And three key tasks always contribute the most.

The Quick List Method

Here is an exercise that we use with our coaching clients very early in the process. We give them a sheet of paper and then tell them, "In thirty seconds, write down your three most important goals in life right now."

We have found that when people have only thirty seconds to write their three most important goals, their answers are as accurate as if they had thirty minutes or three hours. Their subconscious minds seem to go into hyperdrive, and their three most important goals pop out of their heads and onto the paper, often to the surprise of the people doing the exercise.

In 80 percent or more of cases, people have three goals in common: first, a financial and career goal; second, a family or personal relationship goal; and third, a health or fitness goal. And this is as it should be. These are the three most important areas of life. If you give yourself a grade on a scale of one to ten in each of these three areas, you can immediately identify where you are doing well in life and where you need some improvement. Try it yourself and see. Give this exercise to your spouse or your children. The answers can be quite revealing.

Later in our coaching program, we expand this exercise by asking the following questions:

1. What are your three most important *business or career* goals right now?

2. What are your three most important *family or relationship* goals right now?

3. What are your three most important *financial* goals right now?

4. What are your three most important *health* goals right now?

5. What are your three most important *personal and professional development* goals right now?

6. What are your three most important *social and community* goals right now?

7. What are your three biggest *problems or concerns* in life right now?

When you force yourself to ask and answer each of these questions in thirty seconds or less, you will be amazed at the answers. Whatever your answers, they will usually be an accurate snapshot of your true situation in life at the moment. These answers will tell you what is really important to you.

While you are setting goals and priorities, getting organized, concentrating single-mindedly on one task at a time, and disciplining yourself to complete your most important tasks, you must never forget that your ultimate goal is to live a long, happy, and healthy life.

Time Management Is a Means to an End

The main reason to develop time management skills is so that you can complete everything that is really important in your work and free up more and more time to do the things in your personal life that give you the greatest happiness and satisfaction.

Fully 85 percent of your happiness in life will come from happy relationships with other people, especially those closest to you, as well as the members of your family. The critical determinant of the quality of your relationships is the amount of time that you spend face-to-face with the people you love and who love you in return.

The purpose of time management—of eating that frog—and getting more done in less time is to enable you to spend more "face time" with the people you care about, doing the things that give you the greatest amount of joy in life.

**Rule: It is the *quality* of time at work that counts
and the *quantity* of time at home that matters.**

Work All the Time You Work

To keep your life in balance, you should resolve to *work all the time you work*. When you go to work, put your head down and work the whole time. Start a little earlier, stay a little later, and work a little harder. Don't waste time. Every minute that you spend in idle chitchat with coworkers is time taken away from the work that you must accomplish if you want to do well at your job.

Even worse, time that you waste at work often has to be taken away from your family. You have to either stay late or take work home and work in the evenings. By not working effectively and efficiently during your workday, you create unnecessary stress and deprive the members of your family of the very best person you can possibly be.

Balance Is Not Optional

One of the most famous sayings of the ancient Greeks is "Moderation in all things." You need balance between your work and your personal life. You need to set priorities at work and concentrate on your most valuable tasks. At the same time, you must never lose sight of the fact that the reason for working efficiently is so that you can enjoy a higher quality of life at home with your family.

Sometimes people come up to me and ask, "How do I achieve balance between my work and my home life?"

I ask them in return, "How often does a tightrope walker balance when on the high wire?" After a few seconds of thinking, they almost always say, "All the time." I say, "That is the same situation with balance between work and home life. You have to do it all the time. You never reach a point where you have attained it perfectly. You have to work at it."

Your goal should be to perform at your very best at work—to get the very most done and enjoy the very highest level of rewards possible for you in your career. Simultaneously, you must always remember to "smell the flowers along the way." Never lose sight of the real reasons why you work as hard as you do and why you are so determined to accomplish the very most with the time that you invest. The more time you spend face-to-face with the people you love, the happier you will be.

EAT THAT FROG!

1. Determine the three most important tasks that you do in your work. Ask yourself, "If I could do only one thing all day long, which one task would contribute the greatest value to my career?" Do this exercise two more times. Once you have identified your "big three," concentrate on them single-mindedly all day long.

2. Identify your three most important goals in each area of your life. Organize them by priority. Make plans for their accomplishment, and work on your plans every single day. You will be amazed at what you achieve in the months and years ahead.

9

Prepare Thoroughly Before You Begin

No matter what the level of your ability,
you have more potential than you can
ever develop in a lifetime.

JAMES T. McCAY

One of the best ways for you to overcome procrastination and get more things done faster is to have everything you need at hand before you begin. When you are fully prepared, you are like a cocked gun or an archer with an arrow pulled back taut in the bow. You will be amazed at what you achieve in the months and years ahead. You just need one small mental push to get started on your highest-value tasks.

This is like getting everything ready to prepare a complete meal. You set all the ingredients out on the counter in front of you and then begin putting the meal together, one step at a time.

Begin by clearing off your desk or workspace so that you have only one task in front of you. If necessary, put everything else on the floor or on a table behind you.

Gather all the information, reports, details, papers, and work materials that you will require to complete the job. Have them at hand so you can reach them without getting up or moving around. Be sure that you have all the writing materials, log-in information, access codes, e-mail addresses, and everything else you need to start working and continue working until the job is done.

Set up your work area so that it is comfortable, attractive, and conducive to working for long periods. Especially, make sure that you have a comfortable chair that supports your back and allows your feet to rest flat on the floor.

Create a Comfortable Workspace

The most productive people take the time to create a work area where they enjoy spending time. The cleaner and neater you organize your work area before you begin, the easier it will be for you to get started and keep going.

When everything is laid out neatly and in sequence, you will feel much more like getting on with the job.

It is amazing how many books never get written, how many degrees never get completed, how many life-changing tasks never get started because people fail to take the first step of preparing everything in advance.

Launch toward Your Dreams

Once you have completed your preparations, it is essential that you launch immediately toward your goals. Get started. Do the first thing, whatever it is.

My personal rule is "Get it 80 percent right and then correct it later." Run it up the flagpole and see if anyone salutes. Don't expect perfection the first time or even the first few times. Be prepared to fail over and over before you get it right.

Wayne Gretzky, the great hockey player, once said, "You miss 100 percent of the shots you don't take." Once you have completed your preparations, have the courage to take the first action, and everything else will follow from that. The way you develop the courage you need is to *act as if* you already had the courage and behave accordingly.

Take the First Step

When you sit down with everything in front of you, ready to go, assume the body language of high performance. Sit up straight; sit forward and away from the back of the chair. Carry yourself as though you were an efficient, effective, high-performing personality. Then, pick up the first item and say to yourself, "Let's get to work!" and plunge in. And once you've started, keep going until the job is finished.

EAT THAT FROG!

1. Take a good look at your desk or office, both at home and at work. Ask yourself, "What kind of a person works in an environment like this?" The cleaner and neater your work environment, the more positive, productive, and confident you will feel.

2. Resolve today to clean up your desk and office completely so that you feel effective, efficient, and ready to get going each time you sit down to work.

10

Take It One Oil Barrel at a Time

Persons with comparatively moderate powers
will accomplish much, if they apply themselves
wholly and indefatigably to one thing at a time.
SAMUEL SMILES

There is an old saying that "by the yard it's hard; but inch by inch, anything's a cinch!"

One of the best ways to overcome procrastination is for you to get your mind off the huge task in front of you and focus on a single action that you can take. One of the best ways to eat a large frog is for you to take it one bite at a time.

Lao-tzu wrote, "A journey of a thousand leagues begins with a single step." This is a great strategy for overcoming procrastination and getting more things done faster.

Crossing a Great Desert

Many years ago, driving an old Land Rover, I crossed the heart of the Sahara Desert, the Tanezrouft, deep in modern-day Algeria. By that time, the desert had been abandoned by the French for years, and the original refueling stations were empty and shuttered.

The desert was 500 miles across in a single stretch, without water, food, a blade of grass, or even a fly. It was totally flat, like a broad, yellow sand parking lot that stretched to the horizon in all directions.

More than 1,300 people had perished in the crossing of that stretch of the Sahara in previous years. Often, drifting sands had obliterated the track across the desert, and the travelers had gotten lost in the night, never to be found again alive.

To counter the lack of features in the terrain, the French had marked the track with black, fifty-five-gallon oil drums every five kilometers, which was exactly the distance to the horizon, formed by the curvature of the earth.

Because of this, in the daytime, we could always see two oil barrels—the one we had just passed and the one five kilometers ahead of it. And that was exactly what we needed to stay on course.

All we had to do was to steer for the next oil barrel. As a result, we were able to cross the biggest desert in the world by simply taking it "one oil barrel at a time."

Take It One Step at a Time

In the same way, you can accomplish the biggest task in your life by disciplining yourself to take it just one step at a time. Your job is to go as far as you can see. You will then be able to see far enough to go further.

To accomplish a great task, you must step out in faith and have complete confidence that your next step will soon become clear to you. Remember this wonderful advice: "Leap—and the net will appear!"

A great life or a great career is built by performing one task at a time, quickly and well, and then going on to the next task. Financial independence is achieved by saving a little money every single month, year after year. Health and fitness are accomplished by just eating a little less and exercising a little more, day after day and month after month.

You can overcome procrastination and accomplish extraordinary things by taking just the first step, getting started toward your goal, and then taking it one step, one oil barrel, at a time.

EAT THAT FROG!

1. Select any goal, task, or project in your life on which you have been procrastinating and make a list of all the steps you will need to take to eventually complete the task.

2. Then take just one step immediately. Sometimes all you need to do to get started is to sit down and complete one item on the list. And then do one more, and so on. You will be amazed at what you eventually accomplish.

Upgrade Your Key Skills

The only certain means of success is to render
more and better service than is expected of you,
no matter what your task may be.
OG MANDINO

Upgrading your skills is one of the most important personal productivity principles of all. Learn what you need to learn so that you can do your work in an excellent fashion. The better you become at eating a particular type of frog, the more likely you are to just plunge in and get it done.

A major reason for procrastination is a feeling of inadequacy, a lack of confidence, or an inability in a key area of a task. Feeling weak or deficient in a single area is enough to discourage you from starting the job at all.

Continually upgrade your skills in your key result areas. Remember, however good you are today, your knowledge and skills are becoming obsolete at a rapid rate. As Pat Riley, the basketball coach, said, "Anytime you stop striving to get better, you're bound to get worse."

Never Stop Learning

One of the most helpful of all time management techniques is for you to get *better* at your key tasks. Personal and professional improvement is one of the best time savers there is. The better you are at a key task, the more motivated you are to launch into it. The better you are, the more energy and enthusiasm you have. When you know that you can do a job well, you find it easier to overcome procrastination and get the job done faster and better than under any other circumstances.

One piece of information or one additional skill can make an enormous difference in your ability to do the job well. Identify the most important things you do, and then make a plan to continually upgrade your skills in those areas.

Rule: Continuous learning is the minimum requirement for success in any field.

Refuse to allow a weakness or a lack of ability in any area to hold you back. Everything is learnable. And what others have learned, you can learn as well.

When I began to write my first book, I was discouraged because I could use only the hunt-and-peck method of typing. I soon realized that I had to learn to touch-type if I was ever going to write and rewrite a 300-page book. So I bought a touch-typing program for my computer and practiced for twenty to thirty minutes every day for three months. By the end of that time, I was typing forty to fifty words per minute. With this additional skill, I have been able to write more than seventy-five books that have now been published all over the world.

The best news is that you can learn whatever skills you need to be more productive and more effective. You can become a touch typist if necessary. You can become proficient with a computer. You can become a terrific negotiator or a super salesperson. You can learn to speak in public. You can learn to write effectively and well. These are all skills you can acquire as soon as you decide to and make them a priority.

Three Steps to Mastery

First, read in your field for at least one hour every day. Get up a little earlier in the morning and read for thirty to sixty minutes in a book or magazine that contains information that can help you be more effective and productive at what you do.

Second, take every course and seminar available on the key skills that can help you. Attend the conventions and business meetings of your profession or occupation. Go to the sessions and workshops. Sit up front and take notes. Purchase the audio recordings of the programs. Dedicate yourself to becoming one of the most knowledgeable and competent people in your field.

Third, listen to audio programs in your car. The average car owner sits behind the wheel 500 to 1,000 hours each year while driving from place to place. Turn driving time into learning time. You can become one of the smartest, most capable, and highest paid people in your field simply by listening to educational audio programs as you drive from place to place.

The more you learn and know, the more confident and motivated you feel. The better you become, the more capable you will be of doing even more in your field.

The more you learn, the more you can learn. Just as you can build your physical muscles through physical exercise, you can build your mental muscles with mental exercises. And there is no limit to how far or how fast you can advance except for the limits you place on your own imagination.

EAT THAT FROG!

1. Identify the key skills that can help you the most to achieve better and faster results. Determine the core competencies that you will need to have in the future to lead your field. Whatever they are, set a goal, make a plan, and begin developing and increasing your ability in those areas. Decide to be the very best at what you do!

2. Develop a personal plan to prepare yourself to do your most important tasks in an excellent fashion. Focus on those areas where you have special talents and that you most enjoy. This is the key to unlocking your personal potential.

12
Identify Your Key Constraints

Concentrate all your thoughts on the task at hand. The sun's rays do not burn until brought to a focus.

ALEXANDER GRAHAM BELL

Between where you are today and any goal or objective that you want to accomplish, there is one major constraint that must be overcome before you can achieve that major goal. Your job is to identify it clearly.

What is holding you back? What sets the speed at which you achieve your goals? What determines how fast you move from where you are to where you want to go? What stops you or holds you back from eating the frogs that can really make a difference? Why aren't you at your goal already?

These are some of the most important questions you will ever ask and answer on your way to achieving high levels of personal productivity and effectiveness. Whatever you have to do, there is always a *limiting factor* that determines how quickly and well you get it done. Your job is to study the task and identify the limiting factor or constraint within it. You must then focus all of your energies on alleviating that single choke point.

Identify the Limiting Factor

In virtually every task, large or small, a single factor sets the speed at which you achieve the goal or complete the job. What is it? Concentrate your mental energies on that one key area. This can be the most productive use of your time and talents.

This constraint may be a person whose help or decision you need, a resource that you require, a weakness in some part of the organization, or something else. But the limiting factor is always there, and it is always your job to find it.

For example, the purpose of a business is to create and keep customers. By doing this in sufficient quantities, the company makes a profit and continues to grow and flourish.

Every business has a limiting factor or choke point that determines how quickly and well the company achieves this purpose. It may be the marketing, the level of sales, or the sales force itself. It may be the costs of operation or the methods of production. It may be the level of cash flow or costs. The success of the company may be determined by the competition, the customers, or the current marketplace. One of these factors, more than anything else, determines how quickly the company achieves its goals of growth and profitability. What is it?

The accurate identification of the limiting factor in any process and the focus on that factor can usually bring about more progress in a shorter period than any other single activity.

The 80/20 Rule Applied to Constraints

The 80/20 Rule also applies to the constraints in your life and in your work. This means that 80 percent of the constraints, the factors that are holding you back from achieving your goals, are *internal*. They are within yourself—within your own personal qualities, abilities, habits, disciplines, or competencies. Or they are contained within your own company or organization.

Only 20 percent of the limiting factors are *external* to you or to your organization. Only 20 percent are on the outside in the form of competition, markets, governments, or other organizations.

Your key constraint can be something small and not particularly obvious. Sometimes you have to make a list of every step in a process and examine every activity to determine exactly what is holding you back. Sometimes a single negative perception or objection on the part of customers can be slowing down the entire sales process. Sometimes the absence of a single feature can be holding back the growth of sales of a product or service line.

Look into your company honestly. Look within your boss, your coworkers, and members of your staff to see if there is a key weakness that is holding you or the company back, acting as a brake on the achievement of your key goals.

Look into Yourself

Successful people always begin the analysis of constraints by asking the question, "What is it *in me* that is holding me back?" They accept complete responsibility for their lives and look to themselves for both the cause and cure of their problems.

In your own life, you must have the honesty to look deeply into yourself for the limiting factor or limiting skill that sets the speed at which you achieve your personal goals. Keep asking, "What sets the speed at which I get the results I want?"

Strive for Accuracy

The definition of the constraint determines the strategy that you use to alleviate it. The failure to identify the correct constraint, or the identification of the wrong constraint, can lead you off in the wrong direction. You can end up solving the wrong problem.

A major corporation, a client of mine, was experiencing declining sales. The corporation's leaders concluded that the major constraint was the quality of the sales force and the sales management. They therefore spent an enormous amount of money reorganizing the management and retraining the salespeople.

They later found that the primary reason that sales were down was a mistake made by an accountant who had accidentally priced their products too high relative to their competition in the marketplace. Once the corporation revamped its pricing, its sales went back up and it returned to profitability.

Behind every constraint or choke point, once it is located and alleviated successfully, you will find another constraint or limiting factor. Whether you're trying to get to work on time in the morning or build a successful career, there are always limiting factors and bottlenecks that set the speed of your progress. Your job is to find them and to focus your energies on alleviating them as quickly as possible.

Starting off your day with the removal of a key bottleneck or constraint fills you with energy and personal power. It propels you into following through and completing the job. Often, alleviating a key constraint or limiting factor is the most important frog you could eat at that moment.

EAT THAT FROG!

1. Identify your most important goal in life today. What is it? What one goal, if you achieved it, would have the greatest positive effect on your life? What one career accomplishment would have the greatest positive impact on your work life?

2. Determine the one constraint, internal or external, that sets the speed at which you accomplish this goal. Ask, "Why haven't I reached it already? What is it in me that is holding me back?" Whatever your answers, take action immediately. Do something. Do anything, but get started.

13
Put the Pressure on Yourself

The first requisite for success is the ability to
apply your physical and mental energies to one
problem incessantly without growing weary.

THOMAS EDISON

The world is full of people who are waiting for someone to come along and motivate them to be the kind of people they wish they could be. The problem is that no one is coming to the rescue.

These people are waiting for a bus on a street where no buses pass. If they don't take charge of their lives and put the pressure on themselves, they can end up waiting forever. And that is what most people do.

Only about 2 percent of people can work entirely without supervision. We call these people "leaders." This is the kind of person you are meant to be and that you can be, if you decide to be.

To reach your full potential, you must form the habit of putting the pressure on yourself and not waiting for someone else to come along and do it for you. You must choose your own frogs and then make yourself eat them in their order of importance.

Lead the Field

See yourself as a role model. Raise the bar on yourself. The standards you set for your own work and behavior should be higher than anyone else could set for you.

Make a game of starting a little earlier, working a little harder, and staying a little later. Always look for ways to go the extra mile, to do more than you are paid for.

Your self-esteem has been defined by psychologist Nathaniel Branden as "the reputation you have with yourself." You build up or pull down your reputation with yourself with everything you do or fail to do. The good news is that you feel better about yourself whenever you push yourself to do your best. You increase your self-esteem whenever you go beyond the point where the average person would normally quit.

Create Imaginary Deadlines

One of the best ways for you to overcome procrastination and get more things done faster is by working as though you had only one day to get your most important jobs done.

Imagine each day that you have just received an emergency message and that you will have to leave town tomorrow for a month. If you had to leave town for a month, what would you make absolutely sure that you got done before you left? Whatever your answer, go to work on that task right now.

Another way to put pressure on yourself is to imagine that you just received an all-expenses-paid vacation at a beautiful resort as a prize, but you will have to leave tomorrow morning on the vacation or it will be given to someone else. What would you be determined to finish before you left so that you could take that vacation? Whatever it is, start on that one job immediately.

Successful people continually put the pressure on themselves to perform at high levels. Unsuccessful people have to be instructed and pressured by others.

By putting the pressure on yourself, you will accomplish more tasks better and faster than ever. You will become a high-performance, high-achieving personality. You will feel terrific about yourself, and bit by bit you will build the habit of rapid task completion that will then go on to serve you all the days of your life.

EAT THAT FROG!

1. Set deadlines and subdeadlines on every task and activity. Create your own "forcing system." Raise the bar on yourself and don't let yourself off the hook. Once you've set yourself a deadline, stick to it and even try to beat it.

2. Write out every step of a major job or project before you begin. Determine how many minutes and hours you will require to complete each phase. Then race against your own clock. Beat your own deadlines. Make it a game and resolve to win!

14
Motivate Yourself into Action

It is in the compelling zest of high adventure
and of victory, and of creative action that man
finds his supreme joys.

ANTOINE DE SAINT-EXUPÉRY

To perform at your best, you must become your own personal cheerleader. You must develop a routine of coaching yourself and encouraging yourself to play at the top of your game.

Most of your emotions, positive or negative, are determined by how you talk to yourself on a minute-to-minute basis. It is not what happens to you but the way that you interpret the things that are happening to you that determines how you feel. Your version of events largely determines whether these events motivate or de-motivate you, whether they energize or de-energize you.

To keep yourself motivated, you must resolve to become a complete *optimist*. You must decide to respond positively to the words, actions, and reactions of the people and situations around you. You must refuse to let the unavoidable difficulties and setbacks of daily life affect your mood or emotions.

Control Your Inner Dialogue

Your level of self-esteem, how much you like and respect yourself, is central to your levels of motivation and persistence. You should talk to yourself positively all the time to boost your self-esteem. Say, "I like myself! I like myself!" over and over until you begin to believe it and behave like a person with a high-performance personality.

To keep yourself motivated and to overcome feelings of doubt or fear, continually tell yourself, "I can do it! I can do it!" When people ask you how you are, always tell them, "I feel terrific!"

No matter how you really feel at the moment or what is happening in your life, resolve to remain cheerful and upbeat. As Viktor Frankl wrote in his bestselling book *Man's Search for Meaning,* "The last of the human freedoms [is] to choose one's attitude in any given set of circumstances."

Refuse to complain about your problems. Keep them to yourself. As speaker-humorist Ed Foreman says, "You should never share your problems with others because 80 percent of people don't care about them anyway, and the other 20 percent are kind of glad that you've got them in the first place."

Develop a Positive Mental Attitude

In Martin Seligman's twenty-two-year study at the University of Pennsylvania, summarized in his book *Learned*

Optimism, he determined that optimism is the most important quality you can develop for personal and professional success and happiness. Optimistic people seem to be more effective in almost every area of life.

It turns out that optimists have four special behaviors, all learned through practice and repetition. First, optimists *look for the good* in every situation. No matter what goes wrong, they always look for something good or beneficial. And not surprisingly, they always seem to find it.

Second, optimists always *seek the valuable lesson in every setback or difficulty*. They believe that "difficulties come not to obstruct but to instruct." They believe that each setback or obstacle contains a valuable lesson they can learn and grow from, and they are determined to find it.

Third, optimists always *look for the solution to every problem*. Instead of blaming or complaining when things go wrong, they become action oriented. They ask questions like "What's the solution? What can we do now? What's the next step?"

Fourth, optimists *think and talk continually about their goals*. They think about what they want and how to get it. They think and talk about the future and where they are going rather than the past and where they came from. They are always looking forward rather than backward.

When you continually visualize your goals and ideals and talk to yourself in a positive way, you feel more focused and energized. You feel more confident and creative. You experience a greater sense of control and personal power.

And the more positive and motivated you feel, the more eager you will be to get started and the more determined you will be to keep going.

EAT THAT FROG!

1. Control your thoughts. Remember, you become what you think about most of the time. Be sure that you are thinking and talking about the things you want rather than the things you don't want.

2. Keep your mind positive by accepting complete responsibility for yourself and for everything that happens to you. Refuse to criticize others, complain, or blame others for anything. Resolve to make progress rather than excuses. Keep your thoughts and your energy focused forward, on what you can do right now to improve your life, and let the rest go.

15
Technology Is a Terrible Master

There is more to life than just increasing its speed.
MOHANDAS GANDHI

Technology can be your best friend or your worst enemy. Technology becomes the enemy when we give in to an obsessive need to communicate continually. This compulsion to stay plugged in leaves us all psychologically breathless. We have no time to stop, smell the roses, and collect our thoughts.

You Have a Choice

The key is to keep your relationship with technology under control. Bill Gross, who managed more than $600 billion in fixed-income funds and bonds when he was with PIMCO, is famous for exercising regularly and meditating daily to keep centered while using no technology at all. Despite turning off all his devices, he never misses an important message.

For you to stay calm, clearheaded, and capable of performing at your best, detach on a regular basis from the technology that overwhelms you. A researcher who asked a group of CEOs and entrepreneurs to unplug from technology found they had improved memory, deeper relationships, better sleep, and a greater likelihood of making life-transforming decisions.[1]

When people are too plugged in, communications technology quickly becomes a destructive addiction. People wake up in the morning and obsessively check all their phone notifications before leaving their beds. They then race to their computers for yet more typing—before even eating breakfast, drinking water, or brushing their teeth! People are now checking their smartphones about forty-six times each day according to one study[2] and about eighty-five times a day according to another study, which found that "people were accessing their phones twice as often as they thought."[3]

Don't Become Addicted

In Washington not long ago, I was at a business luncheon with a roomful of high-level executives. Prior to the beginning of the luncheon, one of the organizers stood up and said a short grace. All the executives bowed their heads. When the grace was over, the luncheon began.

However, at my table, four or five out of the eight people seemed to have been greatly affected by the prayer. They kept their heads down and their hands in their laps, even when the food was served. They seemed to be lost in deep thought over the profound questions of the day.

Then I realized that they were not praying at all. They were all intensely focused on their smartphones, sending and receiving e-mails, typing like frantic teenagers playing video games. They were all lost to the world around them, drowning in a deep sink full of information exchange.

Take Back Your Time

One of my clients found himself bound and chained to his computer, receiving and responding to e-mails several hours each day. The more time he spent at his computer, the fewer of his other important tasks he was able to get done. The stress caused by these undone tasks, building up like an avalanche overhang, started to affect his personality, his health, and his sleeping habits.

We taught him about the 80/20 Rule and how it applied to e-mails. He deleted and unsubscribed from the 80 percent of his e-mails that had no value. Of the remaining 20 percent, only 4 percent required immediate responses. The other 16 percent could be transferred to an action folder to be worked on later.

Refuse to Be a Slave

Unchain yourself from your computer. Unsubscribe from all unwanted newsletters. Set up an autoresponder that says, "I check my e-mail only twice per day. I will reply as soon as possible. If this is an emergency, phone this number."

A journalist for *Fortune* magazine once wrote that when he arrived back at the office after a two-week European vacation, he had more than 700 e-mails waiting for him. He realized that it would take him a week to get through them all before starting on important projects.

For the first time in his career, he took a deep breath and punched the Delete All button, erasing those 700 e-mails forever. He then got busy with the projects that were really important to him and his company.

His explanation was simple: "I realized that, just because somebody sends me an e-mail, it does not mean that they own a piece of my life." Although not many people would delete their entire in-box, you can definitely delete and ignore more e-mails than you do right now. Empower yourself to remove all e-mails that don't relate to important goals and relationships.

Someone Will Tell You

People often ask me at my seminars, "But don't you have to stay plugged into technology to keep current with the news?" I tell them, "If it is really important, someone will tell you." Many people unplug from the news, and surprisingly enough, they remain well informed on most important subjects. You should do the same.

EAT THAT FROG!

1. Resolve today to create zones of silence during your day-to-day activities. Turn off your computer and your smartphone for one hour in the morning and one hour in the afternoon. You will be amazed at what happens: nothing.

2. Resolve to unplug from technology for one full day each week. By the end of your digital detox, your mind will be calm and clear. When your mental batteries have time to recharge, you will be much more effective at eating frogs.

16
Technology Is a Wonderful Servant

Technology is just a tool.

MELINDA GATES

You must discipline yourself to treat technology as a servant, not as a master. The purpose of technology is to make your life smoother and easier, not to create complexity, confusion, and stress.

Usually, to get more done of *higher* value, you have to stop doing things of *lower* value. Keep asking yourself, *"What's important here?"* What is most important for you to accomplish at work? What is important in your personal life? If you could do only one or two of the activities available to you, which ones would they be?

Use your technological tools to regularly remind yourself of what is most important and protect yourself from what is least important. Technology can be a simple way to get control of your communications, your time, and even your emotions.

Take Control of Your Communication

Clear your digital workspace as you would your physical desk; close every program not needed for the task at hand. Block the websites that distract you the most. Make sure that only the communication channels you need to complete your task are open. Most tasks require some communication, but having ten different ways to communicate is overkill. Once only relevant information is visible on your screen, arrange your windows for perfect workflow.

Show your smartphone who's boss by disabling all notifications—both audio and visual. This is an important step toward checking your phone on your own schedule and thus regaining control of your life.

But What about Emergencies?

Workers with responsibility for young children, elderly parents, or disabled relatives may feel that unplugging from technology or disabling notifications is simply not an option. What if their elderly parent slips in the bath or their young child has an emergency at day care?

This is an absolutely valid concern. The solution, however, is not to be available to everyone at all times. Rather, create a phone number, e-mail address, or other communication channel that only the caretaker of your loved one knows about. Leave that channel open, and reserve it for emergencies.

If you desire, you can do this for your work life as well. Give your boss or key clients a way to reach you that no one else has. You could also program your e-mail manager to automatically sort e-mails from your most important work relationships into a "Read First" folder.

In other words, segment your communication channels so that only frogs can hop into your castle of concentration.

Take Control of Your Time

Your calendar makes a wonderful servant but a terrible master. Never automatically click Accept on a digital invitation. Ask yourself if the invitation really fits your priorities before pressing the button.

Schedule large blocks of time for task completion into your calendar, as if they were appointments. Be so aggressive about it that when people look at your calendar, they will see only a tiny slice of free time. This will impress them and motivate them to schedule shorter meetings.

Your digital to-do list (otherwise known as "task management software") is a powerful tool for taking control of your time. It has all the positives of a paper to-do list plus a few additional features.

Digital to-do lists allow you to transfer items to another person's to-do list at the click of a button. This can help you delegate more efficiently—but make sure you accept only those tasks that are in line with your priorities. A digital to-do list can also be programmed to remind you relentlessly about your most important tasks.

Take Control of Your Emotions Using Technology

Many people fail to make technology their servant because they fear learning new skills. This fear can be mastered: refuse to let it hold you back. Everything is learnable, and what others have learned, you can learn as well.

Let your organization know that you are interested in learning about technological tools that will make you more efficient. If you have a friend, family member, or co-worker who is a tech whiz, learn everything you can from that person.

Above all else, avoid the phrase "I can't." Technology is no longer optional; it is just as important as reading, writing, and arithmetic. And the idea that only certain kinds of people are good at technology is a myth. No matter your age, race, or gender, you have the power to master technology. If you do become frustrated, just remember that it happens to everyone; even expert programmers who are paid hundreds of dollars an hour will sometimes be frustrated by technology.

When you make technology your servant, it can be a source of positive, motivating emotions and increased productivity. Post your most important stretch goal on social media and promise your followers you will achieve that goal. Update them daily on your progress so that if you skip a day or slack off, everyone will know.

Posting on social media about your progress is a great way to reward yourself for making headway on long-term projects. When the payoff is far in the future, it can be hard to stay motivated, so getting likes or hearts from your followers on your daily updates can be a way to achieve a mini-payoff.

You can even seek out people in your field on social media and compete with them to see who can eat the most frogs. For example, many novelists like to share their daily word counts on Twitter so they can see who in their social circle is the fastest and most productive writer—and who gives in to procrastination.

Stop being enslaved by social media, and make it work for you instead. It's simple: instead of posting something trite, post about your life goals and seek the social support to conquer them.

EAT THAT FROG!

1. Resolve today to turn off all notifications, except for your emergency channels. Create special areas in your digital life for your most important tasks.

2. Resolve to research and install one piece of software or one app that will help you be more efficient and focused.

17
Focus Your Attention

All of life is the study of attention;
where your attention goes, your life follows.

JIDDU KRISHNAMURTI

Focused attention is the key to high performance. The "attraction of distraction," the lure of electronic and other interruptions, leads to diffused attention, a wandering mind, a lack of focus, and, ultimately, under-achievement and failure.

Current research proves that continuously responding and reacting to e-mails, telephone calls and texts, and instant messages (IM) has a negative effect on your brain, shortening your attention span and making it difficult, if not impossible, for you to complete the tasks upon which your future and your success depend.[1]

Developing an Addiction

When you check your e-mail first thing in the morning or when you respond to the bell or other sound that indicates an incoming e-mail or message, your brain releases a tiny shot of dopamine. This shot gives you a pleasant "buzz." It stimulates your curiosity and causes you to react and respond immediately. You instantly forget whatever else you were doing and turn your full attention to the new message.

Like the sound of bells ringing when you win while playing a slot machine, the sound of the e-mail or IM triggers the reaction of "What did I win?" You immediately stop your work to find out what your "prize" is.

When you start your day with a few shots of dopamine triggered by your e-mail or IM bell going off, you find it extremely difficult to pay close attention to your important tasks for the rest of the day.

The Multitasking Illusion

Some people believe that they can engage in multitasking, going back and forth between e-mails and important tasks. But people can focus only on one thing at a time. What they are really doing is called "task shifting." They are shifting their attention back and forth, like swinging a searchlight from one object to another.

After an Internet interruption, it takes about seventeen minutes for you to shift your total attention back to your task and continue working. This is precisely why so many people today are working harder and harder, shifting from e-mail interruptions to work and back again, all day long, and getting less and less accomplished. They also make more mistakes.

The Proven Solutions

The solutions are simple and are being adopted by the most productive people in every industry. First, don't check your e-mail in the morning and immediately trigger the all-day dopamine addiction. Leave your devices off.

Second, if you must check your e-mail for any reason, get in and out fast, and get back to work. Turn off the sound on your computer, and put your phone on "vibrate." Stop the stimulations that trigger the flow of dopamine and lead to continuous interruptions.

Finally, resolve to check your e-mail only twice a day, at 11:00 a.m. and 3:00 p.m., and then turn it off again each time. Provide a telephone number where someone can reach you in an emergency.

Whenever you are in a meeting with one or more people, follow the same protocol. Leave electronic devices off. Never insult the persons you are meeting with by working on your laptop or answering your phone. Pay 100 percent attention to the other people. This applies at home as well.

Double Your Productivity

Here is a simple way to double your productivity. First, plan each day in advance, select your most important task, and then start on that task first thing, before you do anything else. Second, work nonstop for ninety minutes with no diversion or distraction, and then give yourself a fifteen-minute break. Third, start again and work another ninety minutes flat out. Finally, after this three-hour work period, you can *then* reward yourself with a shot of dopamine by checking your e-mail.

When you develop the habit of completing three hours of important work each morning, first thing, you will both double your productivity and break yourself of the habit of checking your e-mail all day long. You will regain full control of your life.

EAT THAT FROG!

1. Keep your goals of success and high productivity in mind. Before you do anything, ask yourself, "Is this helping me achieve one of my most important goals, or is this just a distraction?"

2. Refuse to become a slave to the bells and whistles that distract you from completing those tasks that can make a real difference in your life. Leave your devices off.

18
Slice and Dice the Task

The beginning of a habit is like an invisible thread, but every time we repeat the act we strengthen the strand, add to it another filament, until it becomes a great cable and binds us irrevocably, in thought and act.
ORISON SWETT MARDEN

A major reason for procrastinating on big, important tasks is that they appear so large and formidable when you first approach them.

One technique that you can use to cut a big task down to size is the "salami slice" method of getting work done. With this method, you lay out the task in detail, writing down every step in order, and then resolve to do just *one slice* of the job for the time being, like eating a roll of salami one slice at a time—or like eating an elephant one bite at a time.

Psychologically, you will find it easier to do a single, small piece of a large project than to start on the whole job. Often, once you have started and completed a single part of the job, you will feel like doing just one more slice. Soon, you will find yourself working through the job one part at a time, and before you know it, the job will be completed.

Develop a Compulsion to Closure

An important point to remember is that you have deep within you an "urge to completion," or what is often referred to as a "compulsion to closure." This means that you actually feel happier and more powerful when you start and complete a task of any kind. You satisfy a deep subconscious need to bring finality to a job or project. This sense of completion or closure motivates you to start the next task or project and then to persist toward final completion. This act of completion triggers the release of endorphins in your brain, mentioned earlier.

And the bigger the task you start and complete, the better and more elated you feel. The bigger the frog you eat, the greater the surge of personal power and energy you experience.

When you start and finish a small piece of a task, you feel motivated to start and finish another part, then another, and so on. Each small step forward energizes you. You soon develop an inner drive that motivates you to carry through to completion.

"Swiss Cheese" Your Tasks

Another technique you can use is called the "Swiss cheese" method of working. You use this technique to get yourself into gear by resolving to punch a hole in the task, like a hole in a block of Swiss cheese.

You "Swiss cheese" a task when you resolve to work for a specific time period on it. This may be as little as five or ten minutes, after which you will stop and do something else. You will just take one bite of your frog and then rest or do something else.

The power of this method is similar to that of the salami slice method. Once you start working, you develop a sense of forward momentum and a feeling of accomplishment. You become energized and enthusiastic. You feel yourself internally motivated and propelled to keep going until the task is complete.

You should try the salami slice or the Swiss cheese method on any task that seems overwhelming when you approach it for the first time. You will be amazed at how helpful each technique is in overcoming procrastination.

I have several friends who have become bestselling authors by simply resolving to write one page or even one paragraph per day until the book was completed. And you can do the same.

EAT THAT FROG!

1. Put the "salami slice" or "Swiss cheese" technique into action immediately to get started on a large, complex, multi-task job that you've been putting off.

2. Become action oriented. A common quality of high per-formers is that when they hear a good idea, they take action on it immediately. Don't delay. Try it today!

19
Create Large Chunks of Time

Nothing can add more power to your life than concentrating all of your energies on a limited set of targets.

NIDO QUBEIN

Most of the really important work you do requires large chunks of unbroken time to complete. Your ability to carve out and use these blocks of high-value, highly productive time is central to your ability to make a significant contribution to your work and to your life.

Successful salespeople set aside a specific time period each day to phone prospects. Rather than procrastinating or delaying on a task that they don't particularly like, they resolve that they will phone for one solid hour—between 10:00 and 11:00 a.m., for example—and they discipline themselves to follow through on their resolution.

Many business executives set aside a specific time each day to call customers directly to get feedback, to return phone calls, or to answer correspondence. Some people allocate specific thirty-to-sixty-minute time periods each day for exercise. Many people read great books fifteen minutes each night before retiring. In this way, over time, they eventually read dozens of the best books ever written.

Schedule Blocks of Time

The key to the success of this method of working in specific time segments is for you to plan your day in advance and schedule a fixed time period for a particular activity or task. Make work appointments with yourself and then discipline yourself to keep them. Set aside thirty-, sixty-, and ninety-minute time segments that you use to work on and complete important tasks.

Many highly productive people schedule specific activities in preplanned time slots all day long. These people build their work lives around accomplishing key tasks one at a time. As a result, they become more and more productive and eventually produce two times, three times, and five times as much as the average person.

Use a Time Planner

A time planner, broken down by day, hour, and minute and organized in advance, can be one of the most powerful personal productivity tools of all. It enables you to see where you can consolidate and create blocks of time for concentrated work.

During these working times, turn off the telephone, eliminate all distractions, and work nonstop. One of the best work habits of all is to get up early and work at home in the morning for two to three hours. You can get three times as much work done at home without interruptions as you ever could in a busy office where you are surrounded by people and bombarded by phone calls.

Make Every Minute Count

When you fly on business, you can create your office in the air by planning your work thoroughly before you depart. When the plane takes off, you can work nonstop for the entire flight. You will be amazed at how much work you can go through when you work steadily in an airplane, without interruptions.

One of the keys to high levels of performance and productivity is to make every minute count. Use travel and transition times, what are often called "gifts of time," to complete small chunks of larger tasks.

EAT THAT FROG!

1. Think continually of different ways that you can save, schedule, and consolidate large chunks of time. Use these times to work on important tasks with the most significant long-term consequences.

2. Make every minute count. Work steadily and continuously without diversion or distraction by planning and preparing your work in advance. Most of all, keep focused on the most important results for which you are responsible.

20

Develop a Sense of Urgency

Do not wait; the time will never be "just right."
Start where you stand, and work with whatever
tools you may have at your command, and
better tools will be found as you go along.

NAPOLEON HILL

Perhaps the most outwardly identifiable quality of high-performing men and women is action orientation. They are in a hurry to get their key tasks completed.

Highly productive people take the time to think, plan, and set priorities. They then launch quickly and strongly toward their goals and objectives. They work steadily, smoothly, and continuously. As a result, they seem to power through enormous amounts of work in the same amount of time that the average person spends socializing, wasting time, and working on low-value activities.

Getting into "Flow"

When you work on your most important tasks at a high and continuous level of activity, you can actually enter into an amazing mental state called "flow." Almost everyone has experienced this at some time. Really successful people are those who get themselves into this state far more often than the average person.

When you're in the state of flow, which is the highest human state of performance and productivity, something almost miraculous happens to your mind and emotions. You feel elated and clear. Everything you do seems effortless and accurate. You feel happy and energized. You experience a tremendous sense of calm and increased personal effectiveness.

In the state of flow, identified and talked about over the centuries, you actually function on a higher plane of clarity, creativity, and competence. You are more sensitive and aware. Your insight and intuition guide you and direct you to do and say exactly the right things at the right time. You see the interconnectedness of people and circumstances around you. You often come up with brilliant ideas and insights that enable you to move ahead even more rapidly.

Trigger High Performance in Yourself

One of the ways you can trigger this state of flow is by developing a *sense of urgency*. This is an inner drive and desire to get on with the job quickly and get it done fast. It is an impatience that motivates you to get going and to keep going. A sense of urgency feels very much like racing against yourself.

With this ingrained sense of urgency, you develop a "bias for action." You take action rather than talking continually about what you are going to do. You focus on specific steps you can take immediately. You concentrate on the things you can do right now to get the results you want and achieve the goals you desire.

A fast tempo seems to go hand in hand with all great success. Developing this tempo requires that you start moving and keep moving at a steady rate. The faster you move, the more impelled you feel to do even more even faster. You enter "the zone."

Build Up a Sense of Momentum

When you regularly take continuous action toward your most important goals, you activate the Momentum Principle of Success. This principle says that although it may take tremendous amounts of energy to overcome inertia and get started initially, it then takes far less energy to keep going.

The good news is that the faster you move, the more energy you have. The faster you move, the more you get done and the more effective you feel. The faster you move, the more experience you get and the more you learn. The faster you move, the more competent and capable you become at your work.

A sense of urgency shifts you automatically onto the fast track in your career. The faster you work and the more you get done, the higher will be your levels of self-esteem, self-respect, and personal pride. You will feel in complete control of your life and your work.

Do It Now!

One of the simplest and yet most powerful ways to get yourself started is to repeat the words "Do it now! Do it now! Do it now!" over and over to yourself.

If you feel yourself slowing down or becoming distracted by conversations or low-value activities, repeat to yourself the words "Back to work! Back to work! Back to work!" over and over.

In the final analysis, nothing will help you more in your career than for you to get the reputation for being the kind of person who gets important work done quickly and well. This reputation will make you one of the most valuable and respected people in your field.

EAT THAT FROG!

1. Resolve today to develop a sense of urgency in everything you do. Select one area where you have a tendency to procrastinate, and make a decision to develop the habit of fast action in that area.

2. When you see an opportunity or a problem, take action on it immediately. When you are given a task or responsibility, take care of it quickly and report back fast. Move rapidly in every important area of your life. You will be amazed at how much better you feel and how much more you get done.

21

Single Handle Every Task

Herein lies the secret of true power. Learn, by
constant practice, how to husband your resources,
and to concentrate them at any given moment
upon a given point.

JAMES ALLEN

Eat that frog! Every bit of planning, prioritizing, and organizing comes down to this simple concept.

Every great achievement of humankind has been preceded by a long period of hard, concentrated work until the job was done. Your ability to select your most important task, to begin it, and then to concentrate on it single-mindedly until it is complete is the key to high levels of performance and personal productivity.

Once You Get Going, Keep Going

Single handling requires that once you begin, you keep working at the task without diversion or distraction until the job is 100 percent complete. You keep urging yourself onward by repeating the words "Back to work!" over and over whenever you are tempted to stop or do something else.

By concentrating single-mindedly on your most important task, you can reduce the time required to complete it by 50 percent or more.

It has been estimated that the tendency to start and stop a task—to pick it up, put it down, and come back to it—can increase the time necessary to complete the task by as much as 500 percent. Each time you return to the task, you have to familiarize yourself with where you were when you stopped and what you still have to do. You have to overcome inertia and get yourself going again. You have to develop momentum and get into a productive work rhythm.

But when you prepare thoroughly and then begin, refusing to stop or turn aside until the job is done, you develop energy, enthusiasm, and motivation. You get better and better and more productive. You work faster and more effectively.

Don't Waste Time

The truth is that once you have decided on your number one task, anything else that you do other than that is a relative waste of time. Any other activity is just not as valuable or as important as this job, based on your own priorities.

The more you discipline yourself to working nonstop on a single task, the more you progress along the "efficiency curve." You get more and more high-quality work done in less and less time.

Each time you stop working, however, you break this cycle and move back along the curve to where every part of the task is more difficult and time consuming.

Self-Discipline Is the Key

Elbert Hubbard defined self-discipline as "the ability to make yourself do what you should do, when you should do it, whether you feel like it or not."

In the final analysis, success in any area requires tons of discipline. Self-discipline, self-mastery, and self-control are the basic building blocks of both character and high performance.

Starting a high-priority task and persisting with that task until it is 100 percent complete is the true test of your character, your willpower, and your resolve. Persistence is actually self-discipline in action. The good news is that the more you discipline yourself to persist on a major task, the more you like and respect yourself, and the higher is your self-esteem. And the more you like and respect yourself, the easier it is for you to discipline yourself to persist even more.

By focusing clearly on your most valuable task and concentrating single-mindedly until it is 100 percent complete, you actually shape and mold your own character. You become a superior person.

You feel stronger, more competent, more confident, and happier. You feel more powerful and productive.

You eventually feel capable of setting and achieving any goal. You become the master of your own destiny. You place yourself on an ascending spiral of personal effectiveness on which your future is absolutely guaranteed.

And the key to all of this is for you to determine the most valuable and important thing you could possibly do at every single moment and then *Eat That Frog!*

EAT THAT FROG!

1. Take action! Resolve today to select the most important task or project that you could complete and then launch into it immediately.

2. Once you start your most important task, discipline yourself to persevere without diversion or distraction until it is 100 percent complete. See it as a test to determine whether you are the kind of person who can make a decision to complete something and then carry it out. Once you begin, refuse to stop until the job is finished.

Conclusion: Putting It All Together

The key to happiness, satisfaction, great success, and a wonderful feeling of personal power and effectiveness is for you to develop the habit of eating your frog first thing every day when you start work.

Fortunately, this is a learnable skill that you can acquire through repetition. And when you develop the habit of starting on your most important task before anything else, your success is assured.

Here is a summary of the twenty-one great ways to stop procrastinating and get more things done faster. Review these rules and principles regularly until they become firmly ingrained in your thinking and actions, and your future will be guaranteed.

1. **Set the table:** Decide exactly what you want. Clarity is essential. Write out your goals and objectives before you begin.

2. **Plan every day in advance:** Think on paper. Every minute you spend in planning can save you five or ten minutes in execution.

3. **Apply the 80/20 Rule to everything:** Twenty percent of your activities will account for 80 percent of your results. Always concentrate your efforts on that top 20 percent.

4. **Consider the consequences:** Your most important tasks and priorities are those that can have the most serious consequences, positive or negative, on your life or work. Focus on these above all else.

5. **Practice creative procrastination:** Since you can't do everything, you must learn to deliberately put off those tasks that are of low value so that you have enough time to do the few things that really count.

6. **Use the ABCDE Method continually:** Before you begin work on a list of tasks, take a few moments to organize them by value and priority so you can be sure of working on your most important activities.

7. **Focus on key result areas:** Identify those results that you absolutely, positively have to get to do your job well, and work on them all day long.

8. **Apply the Law of Three:** Identify the three things you do in your work that account for 90 percent of your contribution, and focus on getting them done before anything else. You will then have more time for your family and personal life.

9. **Prepare thoroughly before you begin:** Have everything you need at hand before you start. Assemble all the papers, information, tools, work materials, and numbers you might require so that you can get started and keep going.

10. **Take it one oil barrel at a time:** You can accomplish the biggest and most complicated job if you just complete it one step at a time.

11. **Upgrade your key skills:** The more knowledgeable and skilled you become at your key tasks, the faster you start them and the sooner you get them done. Determine exactly what it is that you are very good at doing, or could be very good at, and throw your whole heart into doing those specific things very, very well.

12. **Identify your key constraints:** Determine the bottlenecks or choke points, internal or external, that set the speed at which you achieve your most important goals, and focus on alleviating them.

13. **Put the pressure on yourself:** Imagine that you have to leave town for a month, and work as if you had to get your major task completed before you left.

14. **Motivate yourself into action:** Be your own cheerleader. Look for the good in every situation. Focus on the solution rather than the problem. Always be optimistic and constructive.

15. **Technology is a terrible master:** Take back your time from enslaving technological addictions. Learn to often turn devices off and leave them off.

16. **Technology is a wonderful servant:** Use your technological tools to confront yourself with what is most important and protect yourself from what is least important.

17. **Focus your attention:** Stop the interruptions and distractions that interfere with completing your most important tasks.

18. **Slice and dice the task**: Break large, complex tasks down into bite-sized pieces, and then do just one small part of the task to get started.

19. **Create large chunks of time:** Organize your days around large blocks of time so you can concentrate for extended periods on your most important tasks.

20. **Develop a sense of urgency:** Make a habit of moving fast on your key tasks. Become known as a person who does things quickly and well.

21. **Single handle every task:** Set clear priorities, start immediately on your most important task, and then work without stopping until the job is 100 percent complete. This is the real key to high performance and maximum personal productivity.

Make a decision to practice these principles every day until they become second nature to you. With these habits of personal management as a permanent part of your personality, your future success will be unlimited.

Just do it! *Eat that frog!*

Notes

Chapter 4

1. Andrew Blackman, "The Inner Workings of the Executive Brain," *Wall Street Journal*, April 27, 2014.

Chapter 15

1. Elizabeth Segran, "What Really Happens to Your Body and Brain During a Digital Detox," *Fast Company*, July 30, 2015, http://www.fastcompany .com/3049138/most-creative-people/what-really -happens-to-your-brain-and-body-during-a-digital -detox.

2. Lisa Eadicicco, "Americans Check Their Phones 8 Billion Times a Day," *Time*, December 15, 2015, http://time.com/4147614/smartphone-usage -us-2015/.

3. Lancaster University, "How We Use Our Smart-phones Twice as Much as We Think," *ScienceDaily*, October 29, 2015, https://www.sciencedaily.com /releases/2015/10/151029124647.htm.

Chapter 17

1. Leon Watson, "Humans Have Shorter Attention Span Than Goldfish, Thanks To Smartphones," *Telegraph*, May 15, 2015, http://www.telegraph.co.uk /science/2016/03/12/humans-have-shorter-attention -span-than-goldfish-thanks-to-smart/.

Index

Learning Resources of Brian Tracy International

Brian Tracy
SPEAKER, TRAINER, SEMINAR LEADER

Brian Tracy is one of the top professional speakers in the world, addressing more than 250,000 people each year throughout the United States, Europe, Asia, and Australia.

Brian's keynote speeches, talks, and seminars are described as "inspiring, entertaining, informative, and motivational." His audiences include Fortune 500 companies and every size of business and association.

Book Brian today to speak on one of the following topics:

Business Model Reinvention—How to grow your sales and profitability in any market by analyzing and improving your business model.

High Performance Selling—How to outthink, outperform, and outsell your competition using the most advanced strategies and tactics known to modern selling.

Maximum Achievement—How the top people think and act in every area of personal and business life. Countless practical, proven methods and strategies for peak performance.

Leadership in the 21st Century—How to apply the most powerful leadership principles to manage, motivate, and get better results, faster than ever before.

Brian will carefully customize his talk for you and for your needs. Visit Brian Tracy International at http://www.briantracy.com/speaking/ for more information on how to book Brian for your next event.

Brian Tracy's Online Training Programs— The Keys to Ultimate Success in Any Area of Your Life

Power Productivity with Brian Tracy

If you enjoyed the timeless lessons in *Eat That Frog!*, be sure to check out Power Productivity, Brian Tracy's online training and certification course for time management mastery. This course is designed for those who want to learn, develop, or improve their time management skill set so they can maximize their productivity and achieve greater success in every aspect of life.

To learn more about Power Productivity with Brian Tracy, visit www.briantracy.com/powerproductivity.

Goals Mastery for Personal and Financial Achievement

If you're looking to make true change in your life, consider Goals Mastery for Personal and Financial Achievement, Brian Tracy's ninety-day transformational program that provides you with the clarity and confidence you need to dissolve self-imposed limitations and become an unequivocal powerhouse in the pursuit of your biggest, most important dreams.

To learn more about Goals Mastery for Personal and Financial Achievement, visit www.briantracy.com/goalsmasteryachievement.

How to Write a Book and Become a Published Author

According to Amazon, 82 percent of Americans want to write a book, which is why Brian created his virtual training course, How to Write a Book and Become a Published Author. Using the proven, four-step process that Brian has used to write over seventy of his own books, this program shares an easy-to-follow system for aspiring authors to write and publish their first book.

To learn more about How to Write a Book and Become a Published Author, visit www.briantracy.com/howtowriteabook.

The 6-Figure Speaker

The 6-Figure Speaker is an all-encompassing training course for developing and mastering the art of professional speaking developed by Brian Tracy. This eighteen-part virtual training course is delivered over two consecutive weeks through a sequence of online video modules delivered daily. The course covers everything from powerful speech preparation methods and techniques for overcoming fear to vocal techniques and strategies for negotiating speaker contracts.

To learn more about Brian Tracy's 6-Figure Speaker online virtual training program, visit www.briantracy.com/6figurespeaker.

21st Century Sales Training for Elite Performance

Becoming a master at selling is the single greatest skill you can develop to achieve your personal, professional, and financial goals, which is why Brian created his sales training program, 21st Century Sales Training for Elite Performance. This sales training course is for anyone who wants to move to the top of his or her field, close more sales, make more money, and gain the respect of peers and colleagues as a leader in sales.

To learn more about Brian Tracy's 21st Century Sales Training for Elite Performance program, visit www.briantracy.com/21stcentury.

About the Author

Brian Tracy is one of the top business speakers in the world today. He has designed and presented seminars for more than 1,000 large companies and more than 10,000 small and medium-sized enterprises in 75 countries on the subjects of Leadership, Management, Professional Selling, Business Model Reinvention, and Profit Improvement. He has addressed more than 5,000,000 people in more than 5,000 talks and presentations worldwide. He currently speaks to 250,000 people per year. His fast-moving, entertaining video-based training programs are taught in 38 countries.

Brian is a bestselling author. He has written more than 80 books that have been translated into 42 languages, including *Kiss That Frog!*, *Find Your Balance Point, Goals!, Flight Plan, Maximum Achievement, No Excuses!, Advanced Selling Strategies*, and *How the Best Leaders Lead*. He is happily married, with four children and five grandchildren. He is the president of Brian Tracy International and lives in Solana Beach, California. He can be reached at briantracy@briantracy.com.

books to help you live a good life

Join the conversation and tell
us how you live a #goodlife

@yellowkitebooks
YellowKiteBooks
Yellow Kite Books
YellowKiteBooks